BibleVenture centers™

Jesus—Manger Miracle

Group
Loveland, Colorado

www.group.com

Group resources actually work!

This Group resource helps you focus on **"The 1 Thing™"**—a life-changing relationship with Jesus Christ. "The 1 Thing" incorporates our **R.E.A.L.** approach to ministry. It reinforces a growing friendship with Jesus, encourages long-term learning, and results in life transformation, because it's:

Relational
Learner-to-learner interaction enhances learning and builds Christian friendships.

Experiential
What learners experience through discussion and action sticks with them up to 9 times longer than what they simply hear or read.

Applicable
The aim of Christian education is to equip learners to be both hearers and doers of God's Word.

Learner-based
Learners understand and retain more when the learning process takes into consideration how they learn best.

BibleVenture Centers™: Jesus—Manger Miracle
Copyright © 2005 Group Publishing, Inc.

Visit our Web site: **www.group.com**

Credits
Author: Cheryl Bowen
Editor: Mikal Keefer
Chief Creative Officer: Joani Schultz
Copy Editor: Dena Twinem
Art Director/Designer: Helen H. Harrison
Print Production Artist: John Mestas
Illustrator: Matt Wood
Cover Art Director/Designer: Bambi Eitel
Cover Illustrator: Patti O'Friel
Production Manager: Peggy Naylor

Library of Congress Cataloging-in-Publication Data
Jesus-- manger miracle-- 1st American pbk. ed.
   p. cm. -- (BibleVenture centers)
  ISBN 0-7644-2809-8 (pbk. : alk. paper)
  1. Jesus Christ--Nativity--Juvenile literature. I. Group Publishing. II. Series.

BT315.3.J47 2005
268'.432--dc22

                     2005004995
ISBN 0-7644-2809-8
10 9 8 7 6 5 4 3 2 1   14 13 12 11 10 09 08 07 06 05
Printed in the United States of America.

Contents

Welcome to Bible Ventures™

Ever wish you could connect with *all* your kids—not just the few who seem to naturally enjoy your classroom?

Most Christian educators find themselves wondering why Nancy tracks along with the lesson while Jason is busy poking his neighbors. And why does Darrell light up when it's time to be in a drama, but he'd rather eat worms than do an art project?

If you've wondered if you're a poor teacher or you've got a roomful of aliens, relax. You're dealing with learning styles—and covering all the bases is a challenge every classroom leader faces. You're not alone.

God wired different children differently. That's a *good* thing—otherwise we'd live in a world populated solely by mechanical engineers. Or maybe everyone would be an artist and our world would be a dazzling burst of color and music—but the bridges would all fall down.

We *need* to have different people in the world...and in the church.

BibleVentures gives you the opportunity for hands-on exploration of key Bible events using a variety of learning styles. You'll open up the truth of the Bible Point and the Scripture passage to a wide variety of children, whether they learn best through their ears...their fingers...or their eyes. You'll engage children and provide a "wow!" of surprise as kids move from one BibleVenture Center to another.

And best of all, you'll know that you're helping long-term, high-impact learning to happen. Your kids won't just be *hearing* God's Word; they'll *experience* it. You'll plant it deep in their hearts and minds.

So get ready for a learning adventure. *You'll* know you're providing a balanced, learning experience that taps a range of learning styles, but your kids won't know...or care.

They'll just know they're having a blast learning—and that in your class, you speak their language.

How to Use This Program

Each week children will gather as one large group at **The Depot**—the launching spot for their weekly adventures. Here they'll experience a fun opening that draws their attention to the Bible Point.

From The Depot, children move with their designated group to one of the four **Venture Centers**. Children will remain in their Venture Centers for 40 minutes and while there dive deeply into one portion of the Bible story through dramas, games, music, cooking, or other fun activities. Then everyone returns to The Depot for a time of closing and celebration.

Included in your BibleVentures *book are:*
● 1 leader's section,
● 1 set of leader job descriptions,
● 4 Venture Center leader sections,
● 4 reproducible visa sheets, and
● 1 reproducible CD.

You'll use these resources to lead children on an exciting and interactive four-week journey through the events surrounding Jesus' birth in Bethlehem.

Also included for your use, should you choose to use them, are
● a sample invitation letter to help you encourage kids in your church and your neighborhood to attend, and
● a teacher-training session!

Ready to get started? Here are five simple steps to take as you pull together your BibleVenture Center...

1. Recruit leaders.
You'll need five Venture Center leaders for this BibleVenture.
One leader will oversee The Depot gatherings. The other four leaders will run the four Venture Centers, the learning centers small groups of children will visit. Review the different Venture Centers *before* recruiting leaders; that way you'll be able to match up the major learning style used in each center with someone who enjoys connecting with kids in that way.

For instance, if you have a center that uses lots of music, find a bouncy, fun song leader who loves Jesus and loves kids. If a center uses art to tell a Bible story, ask an artistic, crafty person to lead that center.

Bible Point Alert!

As children move through this BibleVenture program, they'll discover a foundational Bible truth—a Bible Point. The Bible Point is mentioned often in each Venture Center. Encourage your kids to explore the Bible Point and live it out every day of the week!

One plus of the BibleVenture method of teaching is that teachers get to use their strengths! But that only happens if you're careful to match the needs of the centers with the gifts of the teachers.

The person leading The Depot will have new material to present each week, while the Venture Center leaders will teach one session four times over the course of four weeks. Since a new group of children rotates through the center each week, the leader can use the same lesson four times!

This approach allows for less weekly preparation on the part of your center leaders. And they'll improve from week to week as they fine-tune their presentations.

You'll also need some BibleVenture Buddies.

These are adults or capable teenagers who each befriend a small group of children. We call those small groups "Venture Teams." BibleVenture Buddies hang out with their Venture Teams and serve as guides, facilitators, and friends.

BibleVenture Buddies don't prepare lessons or teach. Instead, they get to know their kids. Buddies learn names, pray for the children in their Venture Teams, and reach out to kids in appropriate ways. If Jodie is absent, it's the BibleVenture Buddy who sends a postcard to let her know she was missed. If Jodie is sick, it's her BibleVenture Buddy who calls to encourage her.

BibleVenture Buddies show up for class 10 minutes early so they're ready to greet children. They travel with kids to different centers each week and enthusiastically join in to play the games, do the art project, sing the music, and do whatever else the children do.

Your BibleVenture Buddies aren't teachers, but they help kids connect with the Bible truth being taught in each center. Because they get to know their kids, they're perfectly positioned to help relate the Bible truths to individual kids' lives.

How many BibleVenture Buddies will you need? It depends on how many children participate in your program. For purposes of crowd control and relationship building, it's best if Venture Teams are between five and seven children, and you'll need one BibleVenture Buddy for each group. You'll keep the same groups of children together throughout your four-week adventure.

And here's a tip for leaders: Look for BibleVenture Buddies among people who *haven't* been Christian education volunteers in the past. Clearly communicate that you're not asking these folks to teach; you're asking them to be a friend to a small group of children. This is a completely *different* job than being a Sunday school teacher!

2. Give each leader his or her section of this book.

Don't worry—those sections are reproducible for use in your local church. So

is the CD, so ask a teenager in your congregation to burn a copy for each of the leaders. Copying CDs is easy, inexpensive, and—as long as you use the CDs in your church only—completely legal!

Here's how to distribute the pages:
- The Depot—pages 24-44
- Venture Center One—The Drama Center: pages 45-52
- Venture Center Two—The Art Center: pages 53-62
- Venture Center Three—The Games Center: pages 63-76
- Venture Center Four—The Cooking Center: pages 77-86

3. Create groups of children.

When you're creating individual **Venture Teams**, form your groups with children of various ages. This allows older children to help the younger ones and to be role models. It also results in fewer discipline problems.

"What?" you may be thinking. "Not keep all my third-grade girls together? They'll go on strike!"

Trust us: When you create Venture Teams that combine several ages, *especially* if you have an adult volunteer travel with each group, you'll see fewer discipline issues arise. Children may groan a bit at first, but reassure them that they'll be able to hang out with their same-age buddies before the BibleVenture starts.

Besides, when you use mixed-age groupings, you're also separating your fifth-grade boys!

Some churches choose to create multi-age groups by combining first-through third-graders, and then creating separate groups of fourth- and fifth-graders. This is also an option.

Help children remember what Venture Team they're on by assigning each group a color. Or get into the theme of this BibleVenture and ask Venture Teams to come up with theme-based names for themselves!

As you assign children to their Venture Teams, make a notation on their name tags and on their BibleVenture Visas as to which group they're in. That way, when kids sign in each week at The Depot ticket window, they'll quickly remember what group to join for the remainder of the program.

Be sure each child and adult has a name tag to wear each week. Name tags allow everyone to know each other's names (instead of saying, "You, in the blue shirt") *and* they allow leaders to know that a child has signed in for the day's events. You can make permanent name tags that kids and leaders reuse each week, or write names on self-stick labels. A quick and easy way for kids to know what group they're in is to use name tags in colors that correspond to their Venture Team. Or use white labels and write names in colorful ink that corresponds to Venture Teams.

Please note: Because you have four Venture Centers going at the same time, you need to form four groupings of children to attend them. If you have four Venture Teams, it's easy—just send one group to each Venture Center. If you have more than four teams, do what you can to have an approximately even number of kids (or groups) in each of the centers. It makes life easier for center leaders if they see about the same number of kids each week.

If you have a smaller number of children—fewer than 15—participating in your program, you might consider keeping all the kids together and doing a different Venture Center each week.

4. Make copies of visas.

You'll want a visa for each child in attendance, plus extras for visitors. You'll need them the first time you meet, so run copies now and get that out of the way.

Like the CDs, you can make as many copies as you wish so long as they're used in your local church.

5. Walk through the entire BibleVenture with your volunteers.

Invite your leaders to sit down with you and talk through what they'll be doing, when they'll do it, and where they'll be serving. Many leaders like to know where they'll hold their classes so they can think through the logistics of how to stage a drama or where to store supplies from week to week.

Besides, you'll want to pray with your team and thank them for loving kids and helping kids discover Bible truths. A quick meeting is one good way to do that.

That's it—five easy steps to memorable, exciting, fun learning! BibleVentures is easy—and it's a blast!

During this four-week adventure about Jesus' birth, children will learn John 3:16, which says, "For God so loved the world that he gave his one and only Son, that whoever believes in him shall not perish but have eternal life."

Jesus came to give each person eternal life—and that's good news your kids can share with others!

Children will learn and apply the Venture Verse through activities in The Depot and in the Venture Centers. Consider creating a poster, banner, or other visual with the Venture Verse on it to display during this BibleVenture. Having the verse up front and visible is a boost to memory!

It's important to note that what you're after isn't just that kids can recite the verse—that wouldn't take more than 10 minutes and a stack of candy bar rewards.

What you want is for children to plant the truth of the words deep in their hearts and minds. You want kids to make the connection that Jesus came for us, and because Jesus loves us so much, we live for Jesus and tell others the good news about Jesus.

That's an empowering truth. A truth that may run counter to what children hear on the playground, in class, and—perhaps—at home.

At BibleVentures you won't have children memorize a blizzard of Scripture passages that will be tucked in their short-term memory today and totally gone tomorrow. Instead, kids will be exposed to the meaning of the words—the impact of the truth that God knows them, loves them, and wants to use them as his vessels in their worlds.

If you choose to make Bible memory a larger part of your BibleVenture Centers program, great. It's easy to integrate more verses into the program. But remember that when it comes to bringing about true life change, "less is more." It's far better to focus on one verse that sinks deep into how children view themselves before God than to slide a bunch of words into their heads.

The Venture Visas

Make one BibleVenture Visa for each child. Photocopy the BibleVenture Visas on pages 15-19. Place the cover on top and the pages inside in any order—children won't necessarily move through the program in the order of the visa pages. And have a visa for each child—kids *love* having their own special visas!

Make it easier for kids to know what groups they're in by having the color of each group's construction paper be unique and consistent.

Each week, children will take their BibleVenture Visas with them to their Venture Centers. The leader of each center will affix a sticker to the visa or stamp the visa with a stamp to show children have traveled to that activity. As kids return to The Depot for the closing, leaders will gather the visas and return them to the leader of The Depot, who'll keep them for the following week.

At the last closing, children will receive them to take home.

This visa is the property of

_____

**and secures safe transport
and admittance to each
Venture Center for the bearer.**

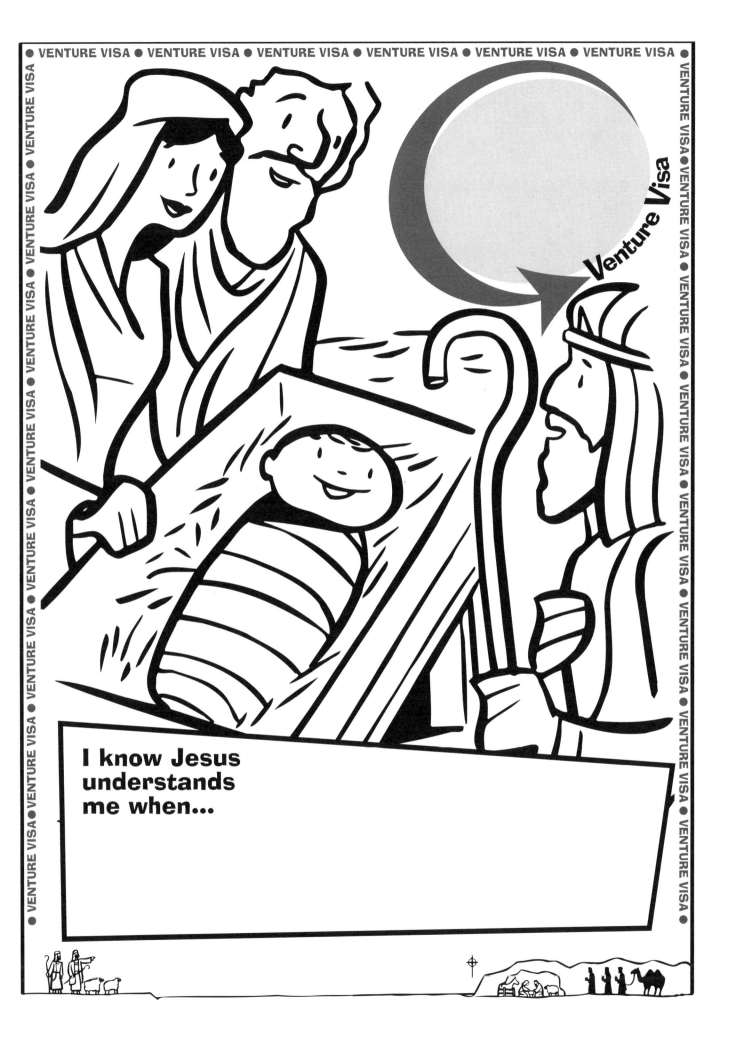

The **Travel Plan**

Use the following chart to help you plan where children will travel each week.

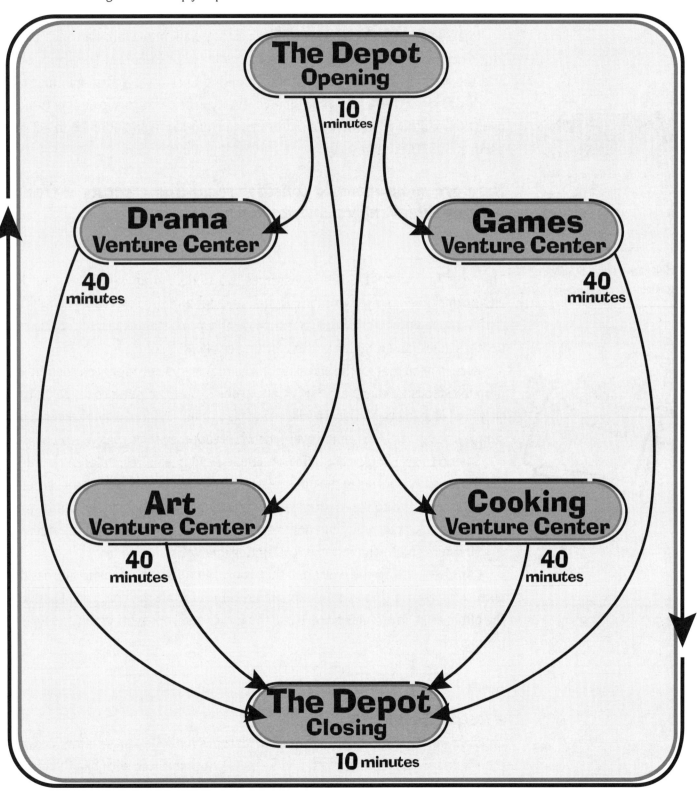

The Depot
Opening

10 minutes

Drama Venture Center

Games Venture Center

40 minutes

40 minutes

Art Venture Center

Cooking Venture Center

40 minutes

40 minutes

The Depot
Closing

10 minutes

You'll be exploring the birth of Jesus for four weeks, so make the most of it and have fun with décor and costumes. You can keep it simple with a few posters or go all out and create an entire Bethlehem landscape.

Imagine the reaction of your children if they walk into a familiar classroom and discover a teacher in a Bible-times costume...or kids find the lights out and the room lit by strings of "stars" (blinking Christmas lights) glimmering overhead...or as they enter your BibleVenture you ask kids to slip simple tunics over their clothing. Suddenly children move from being an audience to actual participants. They're *involved* in the story, not just bystanders.

Here are some ideas to consider regarding creating a fresh, inviting BibleVenture environment:

Costumes

The basis for most Bible-times costumes is a tunic. For an easy-make, quick-wear tunic, fold a length of fabric in half and cut a half-circle from the fold to make an opening for the head. Use a piece of rope or thin length of fabric as a belt. It's quick, and it pulls on over clothing easily.

Keep in mind that for the purposes of your dramas, you need only one definitive prop to establish a character. For instance, while you *could* put a costume on the shepherd characters, all that's really needed is to hand children playing shepherds simple wooden staffs to remind everyone who's supposed to be chasing sheep.

So don't fear simple costuming. A simple headdress gives children the idea they've been transported to the time of Jesus' birth! A set of ears attached to a headband can serve as a donkey costume. The costuming suggestions below assume you have some time and energy, but none of the costumes is especially complicated.

Simple is good—and it makes costuming doable!

Consider putting the word out that you need a few people who are handy with scissors and thread to make simple tunics for all the children. Think of the effort as an investment; you'll use the tunics and rope belts again and again through the years.

Here are some costuming ideas:

● Joseph, Shepherds

Children can wear tunics or bathrobes with ropes for belts. Have children cover their heads with pieces of cloth and keep the cloth in place with headbands of twine or cloth strips. Have children wear sandals or go barefoot.

Check storage areas in your church for old Christmas production backdrops. Also check with people who have been in charge of Christmas programs—costumes may be stored in their attics!

● Mary

Have Mary wear a tunic with a strip of cloth for a belt. Add a shawl over her head and have her wear sandals or go barefoot.

● Angels

Make tunics out of white sheets. If you choose to add wings, a simple approach is to use coat hangers adorned with tinsel. Attach loose elastic straps at the top of the wings—arms can easily slide through the elastic straps to attach the wings to the children.

Scenery

Consider giving your four sessions an extra bit of fun by creating a set in the room where you'll have The Depot segments of your program. You can turn a stage or room into the town of Bethlehem with a few refrigerator boxes and a few cans of spray paint. A couple of sticks outside a "storefront" can support a simple cloth canopy.

Create a set by...

● Painting on large sheets of paper to make backdrops and then tacking or taping the backdrops on the walls.

● To approximate a night scene, attach twinkling Christmas lights to the ceiling and dim or turn off the lights. Children *love* this effect, and lights can be left up throughout this BibleVenture.

● Hang a dazzling star-shaped light over the manger scene.

The Depot

For the next four weeks, you'll lead The Depot portion of our BibleVentures program. Each week, children will gather at The Depot for an opening time and a closing time. Each segment lasts about 10 minutes.

At The Depot, kids sing, review the Venture Verse, and participate in an attention-grabbing experience that introduces the Bible Point. The following lessons will provide all the information you need to have a great time leading this segment of the BibleVenture program!

After the opening, groups of children (Venture Teams) will travel to Venture Centers. Groups of children will stay in the Venture Centers for 40 minutes, then return to The Depot for a time of closing and celebration.

During this BibleVenture, children will learn about the birth of Jesus. Children will discover that (BP) *Jesus came for us and we can share the good news.* That's an important lesson to learn...and put into action!

You'll see the (BP) *Jesus came for us, and we can share the good news* Bible Point mentioned several times in your lessons. That's intentional: Repetition helps children hear and remember. And by the end of this BibleVenture program, children will have considered that Jesus loves them enough to leave his heavenly throne and come to earth for us!

You've been carefully selected to serve in this role. You've got the abilities, attitude, and love of Jesus and kids that it takes to engage and involve children. You'll make good use of those abilities in this program!

Here's a quick outline of your responsibilities as leader of The Depot:

1. Meet and greet kids.
You're the up-front face kids will see each week; it matters how you go out of your way to individually greet as many children as possible. A smile and handshake or pat on the back from you can make a child's day. Because you'll be making the first impression, it's important you arrive *before* children come. You'll also need to set up and recruit someone to distribute the visas each week.

2. Oversee visa distribution.
As children arrive at The Depot, they'll stop at the Depot ticket window to sign in, get their name tags, and pick up their BibleVenture Visas. The ticket window can be as simple as a table with a sign on it, or as elaborate as a booth with a ticket window cut in it.

For an inexpensive, portable booth, set a refrigerator box on end, cut a door in the back, and cut a ticket window in the front. Prime and paint the booth with bright colors, and you'll have a lightweight booth with room inside for one medium-sized adult.

And while you should oversee this function, it's going to be very difficult for you to staff it and take care of everything else that's happening as you lead the program. There will always be children who come a little late and want to sign in while you're up front leading a song.

So unless you can be two places at once, it's important for you to recruit a helper. We call that person the "Servant Leader" because he or she serves you and others—and that's true leadership!

You'll find a job description for the role of Servant Leader on page 95.

3. Set up for the opening—and closing!

The following lessons will tell you everything you need to know. And though the required supplies are simple and easy to find, it will help if you plan ahead.

Again—your life will be far easier if you recruit a Servant Leader to keep the supply cabinet stocked and the sign-in and sign-out organized.

4. Consider inviting a small group of children to learn the songs and lead with you.

This isn't something you *must* do, but if you want to add a little pizazz to the musical portion of The Depot, invite a small group of children to lead the songs with you! You can copy the CDs and send them home with kids so children can learn songs during the week. Then you'll just need a quick 15-minute practice session before The Depot begins.

Children will love being invited to serve as leaders. Their enthusiasm will spread to the other children as well.

5. Consider providing instruments for the kids to add to the songs you sing.

Again—this is by no means required. But if you've already gathered instruments to use in other BibleVentures, pull them out and put them to use in this BibleVenture too!

There isn't a music center in this BibleVenture, but you can still use the instruments in The Depot time during the songs. Provide a few instruments for each BibleVenture Team, or ask volunteers to come up and choose an instrument for specific songs.

Simple rhythm instruments are often easy to find. Look for hand-held cymbals, tambourines, triangle sets, rhythm sticks, maracas or rattles, sand blocks,

or bells. These offer a wide variety of sounds and don't require much in the way of special care.

You may have access to other instruments such as sliding whistles, horns, bells, or harmonicas. Again, be sure these are inexpensive and that the owners (you, the church, or people from whom you borrow the instruments) are OK with the instruments being passed around and treated poorly. This is *not* the time for a church member to loan you an expensive trumpet!

You can also make your own instruments. Fill empty water bottles or plastic eggs with dry rice or beans to make shakers. Wooden dowels or spoons can become rhythm sticks, or use them as drumsticks to tap a beat on an empty cardboard box or a disposable tin pie plate. String jingle bells onto plastic lacing, and tie the string into a bracelet. An empty, round salt carton or oatmeal container can become a bongo drum. Fill a series of glasses with different amounts of water, and let children gently tap these with a metal spoon. Be creative!

If you have instruments that require children to use their mouths, such as harmonicas, horns, or whistles, also provide antibacterial wet wipes. Ask children to clean the mouthpieces of the instruments before and after playing them.

Another cleaning option: Sterisol Germicide and Sanimist Mouthpiece Disinfectant are commercial cleansers available at most music stores.

The Depot

Jesus came for us, and we can share the good news!

Venture Verse: "For God so loved the world that he gave his one and only Son, that whoever believes in him shall not perish but have eternal life" (John 3:16).

Supplies for Week 1

- newsprint
- CD player
-  *BibleVentures: Jesus—Manger Miracle* CD
- markers
- tape
- sticky notes (one pad per Venture Team)
- pens or pencils (3 per Venture Team)

Preparation

Find two children who are willing to say the opening and closing prayers. One way to do this is to ask two BibleVenture Buddies to each select a willing volunteer from his or her group.

Begin playing music from the *BibleVentures: Jesus—Manger Miracle* CD or another age-appropriate, upbeat CD 15 minutes before your scheduled start time.

Post a large, rectangular newsprint banner on the wall at the front of the room. Use markers to write "Good News Herald" in large letters at the top of the banner. That's the name of the newspaper you'll be creating during this BibleVenture. Additional words you write during later meetings will appear as newspaper headlines.

Establish a nonverbal signal to use to direct kids' attention back to yourself. Suggestion: Clap your hands, flick the lights, blow on a wooden train whistle, or use some other unusual sound maker that won't be mistaken in the midst of discussion. Practice the signal several times until kids recognize it and respond to it. A signal that would be especially appropriate for this BibleVenture would be a jingle bell.

Children love recognizing and celebrating birthdays! Take advantage of this enthusiasm by making sure children know you're celebrating Jesus' birthday.

Asking children to lead the prayers will help them gain confidence in praying with other people. Always ask children before the session starts if they are willing to lead. Ask if they'd rather say their own prayer or if they want the words written down for them. If there is no child willing to lead the prayer, then invite an adult to do so.

Protect your walls! Rather than taping newsprint directly to your wall and then writing on the newsprint (markers might bleed through), consider taping paper bags or newspaper to the wall and attaching the newsprint to it.

But be aware that newsprint may mark your walls and require scrubbing to remove the ink. Also, masking tape can remove patches of paint. Consider using painters tape that's designed to not damage paint, or visit a teacher supply store and ask about masking tapes that are friendly to your walls.

The Depot: *Opening*

Welcome children and encourage them to sit with their Venture Teams.

SAY **It's so exciting to begin our journey together here at The Depot! We'll gather here at the beginning and end of each adventure. Since this is the first week of our adventure, I want to be sure you all know what Venture Team you'll be on for this BibleVenture.**

Have each child check his or her name tag, BibleVenture Visa, or other list you've created so children know what Venture Teams they're on. Ask children to sit with their Venture Teams during The Depot.

SAY **We're going to spend the next four weeks celebrating someone's birthday. That's right—four weeks! When it's my birthday, I get a cake and a 30-second song, and that's about it.**

But this birthday is for someone who's extra special! We're celebrating the birthday of God's Son, Jesus.

Each week you'll learn something new about Jesus as you travel to a different Venture Center. And through all our adventures, we'll be reminded that (BP) **Jesus came for us and we can share the good news.**

Jesus came to earth and was born, just like we were all born. But Jesus had a very specific reason for coming to earth: He wanted each of us to have a friendship with God. He came so that could be possible.

Jesus came for each one of us. You're important to God, just like I'm important to God. We're all important to him! And that's good news we can share with others!

Make sure you meet your BibleVenture Buddy. That's the older person who's on your team! Take a moment to check your name tag to be sure it matches your Venture Buddy's name tag.

Now, everyone give your Venture Buddy a high five!

After kids have high fived their Venture Buddies, ask Venture Teams to sit down on the floor. Have children in each group sit in a circle, facing each other.

SAY **Today we're going to play a birthday game. If your birthday is this month, stand up. Great! Happy birthday! Now, sit down.**

If your birthday is in a month that starts with a J, stand up. Happy birthday, you J-month people! Now, sit down.

If your birthday is in a month that ends with a Y, stand up. Happy birthday! Now, sit down.

If you were born on a day that's an odd number, stand up. Happy birthday, you odd people! Now, sit down.

If you were born on a day that's an even number, stand up. Happy birthday, all you even people! Now, sit down.

If your birthday happened on a day that's numbered between 1 and 32, stand up. Happy birthday, everybody! Wish three other people on your BibleVenture Team a happy birthday!

After kids have wished friends a happy birthday,

SAY **Now join me in singing a couple of birthday songs!**

Lead children in singing "Mary's Boy Child" (track 1 on the *BibleVentures: Jesus—Manger Miracle* CD).

SAY **Now let's sing a song that we might remember from when we were little.**

Lead children in singing "Away in a Manger" (track 6 on the *BibleVentures: Jesus—Manger Miracle* CD).

SAY **Maybe you don't think of those songs as birthday songs, but they are. They celebrate Jesus' birthday! Today we're going to discover** 🅱🅿 **Jesus came for us and we can share the good news!**

Ask the children to sit in their BibleVenture Teams.

Give each group a sheet of newsprint and markers.

SAY **If you had really important news to get out to as many people as possible, how would you do it? Brainstorm with your Venture Team as many ways to share your news as possible.**

Give groups two minutes to list or illustrate their answers, then call the groups back together. Ask each person to point an index finger high in the air—after all have raised their hands, ask them to point to the spokesperson for their group!

The lyrics to the songs on your *BibleVentures: Jesus—Manger Miracle* CD are on pages 87-91 of this manual.

The lyrics to the songs on your *BibleVentures: Jesus—Manger Miracle* CD are on pages 87-91 of this manual.

If you'd like to extend your time of worship and singing, lead children in singing one or more of the other songs on the *BibleVentures: Jesus—Manger Miracle* CD.

Give groups a few moments to select a spokesperson, and then ask spokespeople to share their groups' ideas about how to share news. One way to do this in a time-efficient fashion is to start with one team, then ask other teams to offer suggestions that haven't already been noted.

Affirm answers. How you respond to suggestions will determine if you get participation when you later ask for teams to volunteer answers to questions.

SAY **During the time Jesus was born, there weren't lots of ways to get the news out when big things happened.**

Sometimes people posted notices on walls, but there weren't newspapers like we have today. The Internet didn't exist, and television hadn't been invented. (Mention other ways children suggested they would get news out.) **The book of Luke tells us how God chose to announce the good news that Jesus had come to earth as a baby. It involved angels, shepherds, and a star. Not how we'd make an announcement, maybe—but we'll discover how it worked for God during our BibleVenture.**

We'll also discover that BP **Jesus came for us and we can share the good news!**

For now, let's pray together and then head off to an exciting adventure!

Ask the child who you earlier asked to pray to do so at this time. The child can read the following prayer or say his or her own:

"Thank you, God, for sending Jesus to us. He is the greatest gift of all. Be with us as we learn more about your good news! Help us to share your good news with others. In Jesus' name, amen."

Have the leaders of each Venture Center guide the Venture Teams to the area where they'll be meeting. Children will remain at the Venture Centers for 40 minutes. When 35 minutes have passed, signal the Venture Center Leaders to let them know it's time to wrap up their activities and move children back to The Depot for the closing.

The Depot: *Closing*

Play music as children begin entering the room, and allow children to sing as all the Venture Teams return to The Depot. Also, give each BibleVenture Buddy a pad of sticky notes and at least three pens or pencils.

SAY **Welcome back to The Depot! We're singing Christmas songs because we're celebrating Jesus' birthday—and that's what Christmas is really all about! I'm sure each of you had an exciting adventure as you learned about how**

(BP) **Jesus came for us. And just like Jesus came for us, he came for our friends and family members. We can tell all our friends and family about Jesus!**

Lead children in singing "Silent Night" (track 3 on the *BibleVentures: Jesus—Manger Miracle* CD).

Lead children in singing "Mary's Boy Child" (track 1 on the *BibleVentures: Jesus—Manger Miracle* CD).

SAY **Let's imagine Jesus was born today. Maybe his birth would be mentioned in the newspaper. Because he was born in a stable, the evening news would probably carry a brief story about the unusual place Mary gave birth to Jesus. Maybe radio call-in talk shows would take shots at the "heartless innkeeper who denied a room to an expectant mother." *That* topic would get a lot of calls!**

Find a partner in your BibleVenture Team, and discuss this question.

ASK

• If you were a reporter when Jesus was born, what would your headline about Jesus' birth say?

Give pairs two minutes to write one or more headlines on their sticky notes, and then ask pairs to again circle up with their entire BibleVenture Teams. Ask children to share what they wrote with their BibleVenture Buddy and each other.

After groups have had time to hear what kids wrote, ask volunteers to read aloud the headlines they wrote on sticky notes. Invite all kids to stick their headlines on your newspaper. Review some of the headlines together.

SAY **Wow! Those are some great headlines! Next week, we'll check out some ways God got the news out—and some ways we can help get the news out too!**

Lead children in singing "Into My Heart" (track 7 on the *BibleVentures: Jesus—Manger Miracle* CD).

Ask the child who's going to pray to do so. The child can read the following prayer or say his or her own:

"God, we're so grateful that Jesus came for us. Help us to share this good news with others! In Jesus' name we pray. Amen."

Ask children to leave their Venture Visas (and name tags if you've created permanent ones) at the ticket window as they leave. Turn on the CD, and let those children still waiting for their parents join you in singing a few more songs of praise.

Be sure you save the newsprint banner on which children have placed their sticky notes. You'll need it next meeting.

The Depot

Jesus came for us, and we can share the good news! BP

Venture Verse: "For God so loved the world that he gave his one and only Son, that whoever believes in him shall not perish but have eternal life" (John 3:16).

Supplies for Week 2
- Bible
- CD player
- *BibleVentures: Jesus—Manger Miracle* CD
- two 5x7 index cards for each Venture Team
- pair of scissors for each Venture Team
- shawl
- white sheet
- stepladder
- one sticky note for each child
- pencil or crayon for each child
- 1 pen for each BibleVenture Buddy

Preparation
Practice cutting the index card so you're comfortable doing so when it's time to impress your kids by demonstrating the proper "card-cutting" technique.

Add this headline to the newsprint banner you saved from your last meeting: "Angels Bring the Good News: Jesus Came for Us!" Write this in large enough letters that the text is visible to everyone in the room.

Add this headline as well: "Unlikely Group Helps Angels!"

Recruit a teenager or adult to play the part of an angel for the closing session.

As Venture Buddies enter, give each a short stack of sticky notes—one for each child on his or her team—and a pencil or crayon for each child.

Venture view

Asking children to lead the prayers will help them gain confidence in praying with other people. Always ask children before the session starts if they are willing to lead. Ask if they'd rather say their own prayer or if they want the words written down for them. If there is no child willing to lead the prayer, then invite an adult.

Find two children who are willing to offer the opening and closing prayers. One way to do this is to ask two BibleVenture Buddies to each select a willing volunteer from his or her team. If you can't find children willing to do this, don't push the issue. Instead, ask Venture Buddies to serve in this way.

Begin playing music from the *BibleVentures: Jesus—Manger Miracle* CD or another age-appropriate, upbeat CD 15 minutes before your scheduled start time. You'll welcome the children to an exciting place!

The Depot: *Opening*

Welcome children and encourage them to sit with their Venture Teams. Be sure that children who were not here last week know which Venture Teams to join and are welcomed warmly.

As they enter, give each Venture Buddy two index cards, a pair of scissors, and a pen. Also, be sure to distribute to each Venture Buddy a sticky note and a crayon or pencil for each child on his or her team.

Ask Venture Teams to sit down on the floor. Have children in each group sit in a circle, facing each other.

SAY **It's time to celebrate some birthdays! If you know for certain you were born during the day, stand up. Happy birthday, you daylight people! Now everyone sit down.**

If you know for certain you were born at night, stand up. Happy birthday, you night owls! Now sit down.

If you know for certain you were born sometime either in the light or dark, stand up. Happy birthday, everybody!

Give two other people who were born about the same time you were a high five. You've got 20 seconds!

After 20 seconds, draw everyone's attention back to you.

SAY **It's fun to celebrate birthdays together. Today we'll celebrate someone else's birthday who was born a long time ago—Jesus! Let's sing together about Jesus!**

Lead children in singing "Mary's Boy Child" (track 1 on the *BibleVentures: Jesus—Manger Miracle* CD) and "My Jesus, I Love Thee" (track 10).

SAY **I gave each BibleVenture Buddy two cards. One is to use later, so tuck it away. Use the other to meet this challenge: Find a way to have one member of your team walk *through* the card.**

Give teams several minutes to brainstorm and try ideas. If no one accomplishes this task, demonstrate how to cut the card so it opens up and a child can walk through the opening. See the diagram in the margin for details.

SAY **Now, this was just a trick, but the Bible records many things God's done that seemed impossible, like it seemed impossible to walk through a small card**.

Ask children to sit with their teams and together name as many of the Bible's miracles as the children can remember in 90 seconds. Ask BibleVenture Buddies to make a list on the second card.

After 90 seconds, ask teams to call out one miracle at a time, without repeating, until they've run out of ideas.

SAY **Let's look at a Bible story that's full of news that seemed impossible! I need three volunteers to help me act out a play.**

Choose volunteers to play the parts of Gabriel, Mary, and the narrator.

Before asking the narrator to read Luke 1:26-38 aloud, position Mary in a chair and Gabriel several steps up the stepladder. Put a shawl around Mary's shoulders and the white sheet around the angel (think toga!).

Instruct Mary and Gabriel to mime their parts with enthusiasm as the narrator reads the Bible passage clearly and with feeling.

After the passage has been read and acted, lead kids in a round of applause for your volunteers.

Preselect a capable reader to be the narrator. Don't risk embarrassing a child who's uncomfortable reading in public or who can't deliver the reading clearly and with emotion.

SAY **In your Venture Team, discuss these questions.**

ASK

• **What would your face look like if an angel came to talk to you? Show your Venture Buddy!**

• **When Mary heard the angel's news, how do you think she felt? Why?**

SAY **Mary was faithful, even though at first she may have been startled. Let's sing a song about being faithful!**

 Lead children in singing "O Come, All Ye Faithful" (track 5 on the *BibleVentures: Jesus—Manger Miracle* CD).

 Lead children in singing "Silent Night" (track 3 on the *BibleVentures: Jesus—Manger Miracle* CD).

Ask the child who's going to pray to do so. The child can read the following prayer or say his or her own:

"God, we thank you because Jesus came for us! Help us learn to be faithful like Mary! Teach us how to share your good news! Let us grow closer to you today! Amen."

Have the leaders of each Venture Center guide the Venture Teams to the area where they'll be meeting. Children will remain at the Venture Centers for 40 minutes. When 35 minutes have passed, signal the Venture Center leaders to let them know it's time to wrap up their activities and move children back to The Depot for the closing.

The Depot: *Closing*

As children begin entering the room, lead them in singing "O Come, All Ye Faithful" (track 5 on the *BibleVentures: Jesus—Manger Miracle* CD).

SAY **Welcome back to The Depot! Did you have fun in your centers today? I'm glad! We want you to have a good time as you're discovering that (BP) Jesus came for us and we can share the good news!**

At this point, have the actor who's playing the part of an angel burst into the room and say: Have you heard about the baby? God's Son is born! Jesus has come! We get to share the news! Are you angels? Come help us get the news out! Straighten up your wings—it's time to share the news! Let's sing to the baby!

Lead children in singing "Joy to the World" (track 2 on the *BibleVentures: Jesus—Manger Miracle* CD).

The angel will then say: "Wow! You have great voices! You'll be a big help getting the word out. Let's tell the shepherds now. Ready to try your wings? We've got to get over to the fields to talk to those shepherds!"

The angel will lead the children in "soaring" with their arms for a few seconds.

Then the angel will say: "Now watch their faces when they look up and see me. Scared shepherds make the funniest faces."

Talking to an imaginary group of shepherds down below, the angel will say: "Hey, shepherds, Jesus has come for us! He's in Bethlehem in a manger, wrapped in swaddling clothes."

The angel will turn to the children again and say: "Sing with me so they'll understand."

Lead children in singing "O Come, All Ye Faithful" (track 5 on the *BibleVentures: Jesus—Manger Miracle* CD).

The angel will then say: "Look at those shepherds running for the city! They're going to go see baby Jesus, and then they'll tell lots of people the good news. Thanks for your help! Remember 🅑🅟 Jesus has come, and we can share the good news. See you later!"

The angel will then exit.

SAY **Did you like being an angel for a few minutes? It must have been exciting for the shepherds to share that Jesus came for us. That's good news we can still share today, you know. There are lots of people who haven't heard it yet.**

Circle up with your Venture Team, and pretend you get to write a 30-second radio commercial that tells the world about the birth of Jesus. What would you say in 30 seconds? You'll have just three minutes to write your commercial.

Give groups three minutes to create a commercial. After three minutes have passed, ask some of the groups to share their thoughts.

SAY **Those are great ideas! Now circle up in your Venture Teams again. BibleVenture Buddies, give a sticky note and crayon or pencil to each member of your group.**

On that sticky note, write one word that describes how you think the shepherds felt when angels appeared with the good news about Jesus. Share what you wrote in your Venture Teams, then bring your sticky notes up to put on our newspaper.

Allow kids time to write then bring their sticky notes and put them on the newspaper.

SAY **Let's sing a song as a prayer.**

💿 Lead children in singing "Into My Heart" (track 7 on the *BibleVentures: Jesus—Manger Miracle* CD).

SAY **It's been great discovering that Jesus came for us. Let's remember this week that we can share with others the good news about Jesus coming!**

Ask children to leave their Venture Visas (and name tags if you've created permanent ones) at the ticket window as they leave. Turn on the CD, and let those children still waiting for their parents join you in singing a few more songs of praise.

Be sure you keep the newsprint banner on which children have placed their sticky notes. You'll need it next meeting.

Ask the child who agreed to offer a closing prayer to do so now.

The Depot

Jesus came for us, and we can share the good news!

Venture Verse: "For God so loved the world that he gave his one and only Son, that whoever believes in him shall not perish but have eternal life" (John 3:16).

Supplies for Week 3
- Bible
- CD player
- *BibleVentures: Jesus—Manger Miracle* CD

Preparation

Add this headline to the newsprint banner you saved from your last meeting: "Star Leads Wise Men to the Greatest Gift! Jesus Came for Us!" Write this in large enough letters that the text is visible to everyone in the room.

Ask a child to lead prayer for the opening.

If you choose to have a birthday party at your next meeting, make one copy of the invitation (page 112) for each child.

The Depot: *Opening*

Welcome children and encourage them to sit with their Venture Teams. Be sure that children who were not here last week know which Venture Teams to join and are welcomed warmly.

Ask Venture Teams to sit on the floor. Have children in each group sit in a circle, facing each other.

SAY **It's time to celebrate some birthdays!**

If you were born at home, stand up. Happy birthday, you homebodies! Now sit down.

If you were born in a hospital, stand up. Happy birthday, you hospital babies! Now sit down.

If you were born in a car on the way to the hospital, stand up. Happy birthday, you early arrivals!

Send the birthday party invitations home this week with parents so that they can come a few minutes early next week and celebrate Jesus' birthday during the closing time.

If you hold your BibleVenture at a time there are other classes meeting in your church, consider also inviting one or two classes to join you for the closing celebration birthday party.

If you don't really remember where you were when you were born, but you're pretty sure you were with your mother, stand up. Happy birthday!

Give a high five to five other people in the room you haven't seen this week!

SAY **Happy birthday! It is great to celebrate birthdays together. We're celebrating Jesus' birthday today too. Let's sing together about Jesus!**

Lead children in singing "Mary's Boy Child" (track 1 on the *BibleVentures: Jesus—Manger Miracle* CD).

SAY **The last few times we met together, we talked about ways God shared the good news that Jesus came for us. There were angels, and shepherds, and a star. I want to read you what the Bible says about that star.**

Read aloud Matthew 2:1-2, 9-11.

SAY **That must have been some bright star! Circle up in your Venture Team, sitting on the floor knee to knee. I want you to do something for me.**

After kids have formed circles,

SAY **Starting with the person who's wearing the most white (because I always think of stars twinkling white in the sky), go around your circle and think of words that describe Jesus that start with the letters S, T, A, and R. For instance, the letter S might remind me that Jesus is my *Savior*...or that Jesus *served* others. Those are words that start with the letter S that remind me of Jesus.**

Go around your circle spelling the word *star* over and over. See if you can spell *star* at least four times before you run out of words. Help each other if you get stuck!

After most groups are beginning to struggle for words, continue.

SAY **The wise men who followed the star so they could locate a new king found just what they were looking for. Jesus *is* a king—and he came for us! Let's sing a song about the wise men. Stand, and join me in singing, please.**

Lead children in singing "Three Wise Men" (track 4 on the *BibleVentures: Jesus—Manger Miracle* CD).

SAY **Now let's sing a quiet song so we can get ready to pray together.**

Lead children in singing "Jesus Is All the World to Me" (track 8 on the *BibleVentures: Jesus—Manger Miracle* CD).

Ask the child who's going to pray to do so. The child can read the following prayer or say his or her own:

"God, thank you for good gifts. We especially thank you for the best gift of all. That's Jesus, who came for us. Help us to share the good news with others! In Jesus' name we pray. Amen."

Have the leaders of each Venture Center guide the Venture Teams to the area where they'll be meeting. Children will remain at the Venture Centers for 40 minutes. When 35 minutes have passed, signal the Venture Center leaders to let them know it's time to wrap up their activities and move children back to The Depot for the closing.

The Depot: *Closing*

 As children begin entering the room, lead them in singing "Three Wise Men" (track 4) and "Joy to the World" (track 2 on the *BibleVentures: Jesus—Manger Miracle* CD).

SAY **Welcome back to The Depot! The Bible tells us the wise men followed a star to find out about Jesus. Circle up with your Venture Team and discuss these questions.**

ASK

• **How do people find out about Jesus today?**

• **How did you find out about Jesus?**

Allow adequate time for discussion, then ask groups to also discuss the following question.

ASK

• **What's easy or hard about telling friends about Jesus?**

When you have about two minutes until it's time for you to dismiss, use your attention-getting signal to draw Venture Teams' attention back to you.

SAY **Venture Buddies, please send a member of your Venture Team up to pick up a copy of our invitation for each person in your group.**

Distribute these if you'll be inviting parents to join you for a celebration next week. As they're distributed to children, encourage kids to ask their parents to come early the following week so they can join in the fun. If you won't be having a party at next week's closing, don't mention the invitations. An invitation you can complete and copy is on page 112.

SAY **Please pray with me.**

PRAY **Jesus, we love you. We are so glad that you came for us. You are such a precious gift. We want to give good gifts back to you, too, and those gifts are our hearts. Amen.**

Ask children to leave their Venture Visas (and name tags if you've created permanent ones) at the ticket window as they leave. Turn on the CD, and let those children still waiting for parents join you in singing a few more songs of praise.

Be sure you keep the newsprint banner on which children have placed their sticky notes.

Week 4 — The Depot

Jesus came for us, and we can share the good news! (BP)

Venture Verse: "For God so loved the world that he gave his one and only Son, that whoever believes in him shall not perish but have eternal life" (John 3:16).

Supplies for Week 4

- CD player
- *BibleVentures: Jesus—Manger Miracle* CD
- birthday cupcakes—one per child, Venture Buddy, and visitor
- paper napkins
- streamers
- balloons

Preparation

Ask several adults or teenagers to help you during the closing when you're serving snacks.

Find two children who are willing to say the opening and closing prayers. One way to do this is to ask two BibleVenture Buddies to each select a willing volunteer from his or her group.

Add this headline to the newspaper: "Shepherds Run Wild in Bethlehem Streets!"

For the closing, add this headline: "Great Time Had at BibleVenture. Here's How!"

While children are busy at the Venture Centers, decorate your Depot area as if for a birthday party, using streamers and balloons.

Place cupcakes and party supplies out of the children's sight.

Begin playing music from the *BibleVentures: Jesus—Manger Miracle* CD or another age-appropriate, upbeat CD 15 minutes before your scheduled start time.

The Depot: *Opening*

SAY **Welcome to The Depot! Let's celebrate some birthdays!**

Lots of parents send out birth announcements when their children are born. If, when you were born, the announcements probably read "It's a girl," stand up. Happy birthday, you girls! Now sit down.

If the birth announcement probably read "It's a boy," stand up. Happy birthday, guys! Now sit down.

If the announcement probably read "It's a cute kid," stand up. Happy birthday, you cute kids! Now give high fives to five *other* cute kids!

After kids have delivered their high fives,

SAY It's fun to celebrate birthdays, and today we're celebrating Jesus' birthday. Let's sing a birthday song about the birth of Jesus!

Lead children in singing "Joy to the World" (track 2 on the *BibleVentures: Jesus—Manger Miracle* CD).

SAY Huddle up with your BibleVenture Buddies, and think of three ways God chose to share the good news about Jesus' birth. You've got 18 seconds!

After 18 seconds have passed, point to different Venture Buddies and ask them to call out what they heard in their groups. Ask Venture Buddies to mention just ideas that haven't already been mentioned.

SAY Angels...a star...shepherds...God got the word out, didn't he? And you'd think by now everyone in the world would have heard the good news about Jesus...but they haven't.

The shepherds ran into the closest town to see Jesus and to tell people the good news that Jesus came for us. We can share that good news in our town too!

If God let shepherds share that (BP) Jesus came for us, do you think we can share the good news too? Circle up with your Venture Team, and let's talk about that.

After kids are sitting in circles with their Venture Buddies, ask groups to discuss these questions.

ASK

• Whose job is it to tell our town about Jesus? Why?

• How can we tell our town about Jesus?

• What is it we need to share about Jesus?

When you have about one minute before it's time to release kids to the Venture Centers, draw attention back to yourself.

SAY This is the last day of our BibleVenture. We've discovered that (BP) Jesus came for us and we can share the good news. That's great! Let's celebrate that when we come back together for our closing!

Ask the child who's going to pray to do so. The child can read the following prayer or say his or her own:

"God, thank you that Jesus came for each of us. Thank you that you love each of us. Help us to share this good news with others. Amen."

Have the leaders of each Venture Center guide the Venture Teams to the area where they'll be meeting. Children will remain at the Venture Centers for 40 minutes. When 35 minutes have passed, signal the Venture Center leaders to let them know it's time to wrap up their activities and move children back to The Depot for the closing.

The Depot: *Closing*

SAY **Welcome back to The Depot! You've invited some guests, so be sure you say hello and let them know you're glad they joined us. Let's take one minute to do that now.**

After a minute has passed, continue.

SAY **Guests, join a BibleVenture Team at this time. You can bring a chair to sit with a group. BibleVenture Teams, introduce yourselves to your visitors, and tell one thing you've loved about this BibleVenture!**

Allow time for these activities.

SAY **We invited guests today because we've been making discoveries about the birth of Jesus. We found lots of ways God shared the good news about Jesus. We've learned we can share the good news, too, and we want to share that news with you! Let's join together in singing two birthday songs about Jesus.**

Start earlier than usual to be ready for this closing. You want everything prepared as the visitors and children enter the room. Be sure that the music is playing 15 minutes before beginning time and that the rest of your supplies are in the back of the room. Be sure to greet visitors if they arrive first, and let them know that the children will be here soon.

Lead children in singing "Joy to the World" (track 2 on the *BibleVentures: Jesus—Manger Miracle* CD).

Lead children in singing "Away in a Manger" (track 6 on the *BibleVentures: Jesus—Manger Miracle* CD).

Ask the child who's going to pray to do so. The child can read the following prayer or say his or her own:

"Dear God, thank you for loving us so much that you sent Jesus for us. Help us to share this good news with others. Thank you for our visitors. Bless the food that we share together. In Jesus' name, amen."

SAY **We've talked about Christmas being Jesus' birthday, so let's celebrate with some traditional birthday snacks: cupcakes!**

If your children are sitting on the floor during The Depot, you may want to add some chairs around the walls of the room for your visitors. Adults won't be dressed for sitting on the floor, and many older people don't have enough mobility to get up from the floor without difficulty.

Ask a volunteer to bring out the cupcakes.

SAY **We've had lots of fun at our BibleVenture! As we share cupcakes together, tell your visitors what you've done in the BibleVenture centers so far.**

If you chose not to have visitors join you, simply ask children to tell each other what they've enjoyed about the BibleVenture meetings.

When you have about three minutes before closing, draw attention to yourself, and invite everyone to join you in singing another birthday song—this one for each person in the room who has a birthday.

Lead children in singing "We're So Glad That You Were Born" (track 9 on the *BibleVentures: Jesus—Manger Miracle* CD).

SAY **Kids, as you leave today, take your Venture Visas with you. Your Visa will be a reminder of the travels you've had in this BibleVenture. Whenever you see your Venture Visa, you'll remember that (BP) Jesus came for us and we can share the good news with others!**

Venture Center One:

The Drama Center

Jesus came for us, and we can share the good news!

Venture Verse: "For God so loved the world that he gave his one and only Son, that whoever believes in him shall not perish but have eternal life" (John 3:16).

Welcome!

You'll be leading the Drama Venture Center for the next four weeks.

One great piece of news is that preparing for the four weeks is easy because you prepare just one week's lesson—and present it four times!

Here's how your Venture Center works. Each week children gather at The Depot for a time of opening and adventure. While at The Depot, children will get together with their Venture Teams, and then one group (it could be one Venture Team or several, but each will have an adult or teenage leader) will travel to your Venture Center.

This group of children will stay with you for 40 minutes then return to The Depot for a time of closing and celebration.

In the weeks that follow, different groups of children will come to your Venture Center. You'll repeat the same activity for all four weeks, each week with a different group of children. This allows you to prepare just once and have four weeks of meaningful interaction with children as you lead them closer to God!

Your Venture Center

During this BibleVenture, children explore the birth of Jesus. Children will learn that BP Jesus came for us and we can share the good news.

You'll notice that the Point, BP Jesus came for us, and we can share the good news, is mentioned several times in your lesson. That's by intent, and it's important you reinforce the Point by saying it each time—or even more often. By the end of this BibleVenture, children will have learned about the Christmas story and considered how they can respond to God's great gift.

In your Venture Center, children will use drama to discover more about the birth of Jesus. For the children, there's no memorizing lines or turning script pages; children simply experience the story through the eyes of a shepherd who

takes them on a journey as he recalls that amazing night.

Your enthusiasm for this Venture Center and the drama will be passed on to the children you meet each week. Greet them with excitement, be the first to be amazed by the shepherd, encourage them to join into the drama, and have fun!

And be sure that you read ahead and plan for your Venture Center. Planning ahead and arriving early are both keys to leading a successful center!

Preparation

Before children arrive, gather these supplies:
- Bible
- 2 CD players
- 2 copies of *BibleVentures: Jesus—Manger Miracle* CD
- manger (or box covered with old blanket)
- doll
- scraps of blankets to wrap the doll
- a little hay for the manger
- small votive candles in safe containers
- matches or lighters
- an appropriate sticker or stamp to use in each child's Venture Visa
- twinkling, small, clear Christmas tree lights
- Bible-times costumes for the shepherd, Mary, and Joseph. Include robes, sashes, and sandals. For more costume ideas, see pages 22-23.

Recruit three people to play dramatic roles (you can be one of the actors if necessary). You'll need actors for these three characters:

1. **Shepherd:** This actor will need a costume and must memorize or be very familiar with the script.

2. **Mary:** This actor will need a costume, and when children leave your room to go with the "Shepherd," "Mary" will quickly set up a Nativity scene, turn on Christmas lights, place and light candles, turn off the room's electric lights, and then sit quietly.

3. **Joseph:** This actor will need a costume, and when children leave your room to go with the Shepherd, "Joseph" will help Mary with arrangements as well as play track 13 of the *BibleVentures: Jesus—Manger Miracle* CD on a CD player set to "repeat."

Place the manger (containing hay and a doll) where children won't see it. Also, hide the candles, matches, and actors.

If you like, videotape part or all of the drama. Kids won't have time to watch themselves enact the whole drama during this Venture Center, but you may have time to show them a portion of it before they return to The Depot.

At least one week in advance, give the actor playing the Shepherd the script to memorize. Determine where the costumed actors will be during the opening celebration so children don't see them.

Select a spot for the Shepherd to take the children while he tells his story. Be sure to reserve that area so it's clear and available when your Shepherd leads children there. Find a hidden place in that area to put a CD player.

Attach the Christmas tree lights to the ceiling in your meeting room in as inconspicuous a way as possible. You don't want children to pay attention to the lights until you're ready to light them.

You'll need to use the *BibleVentures: Jesus—Manger Miracle* CD in two places, so burn copies of the CD for your use.

Please note that the scripts match what you'll hear on the CD.

Set up a stage area. This may be one side of the room or an actual stage.

The Venture Center

Welcome children as they enter your Venture Center. Explain that kids will explore the events surrounding Jesus' birth by getting involved in a drama. As groups enter your BibleVenture area, move them away from the doorway and ask them to sit down on the floor.

SAY **We're going to look at what may be a familiar passage of Scripture. We'll look at an account found in Luke, a book that's in the Bible.**

Luke gives us a pretty complete report about events surrounding Jesus' birth in Bethlehem. What's great is that when you read about Jesus' birth you quickly see that Jesus came for us and we can tell others the good news!

Here's what the book of Luke says...

Open your Bible and begin reading aloud at Luke 2:1.

After you've read the first verse, the actor portraying the Shepherd will burst into the room. The Shepherd will then present the Bible material in a dramatic form, with your children playing the part of Associate Shepherds.

Use the following script.

Shepherd:

Wow—you people are *never* going to believe what I've seen! The Messiah, the Lord—he's here! He was born last night in Bethlehem. I've seen him, the child promised by the prophets!

Establish a nonverbal signal to direct kids' attention back to yourself. Suggestions: Clap your hands, flick the lights, or blow on a wooden train whistle or other unusual sound maker that won't be mistaken in the midst of discussion. Practice the signal several times until kids recognize it and respond to it.

Consider stringing several large "jingle bells" together to serve as a signal in this center. They're bright, cheery, and seasonal!

Here are some possible places the Shepherd can take your Venture Teams: an empty classroom, a stairwell landing (with children sitting on the stairs and the Shepherd at the bottom), a wide hallway, an unoccupied corner of the fellowship hall—anywhere far enough away from your meeting space to feel like the kids made a journey with the Shepherd.

And be sure your Shepherd is an enthusiastic storyteller! Children will experience the Bible story through his or her eyes, so select someone who can paint vivid word pictures.

Me and some other shepherds were outside of town, over on the slope that's…hey, you guys are shepherds, too, right?

You look like shepherds—all scruffy-like.

And you *smell* like shepherds…us shepherds don't take baths too often. We want the sheep to be able to find us in the dark.

What I don't understand is why there are so many shepherds here and yet—there are no sheep. What's *wrong* with you shepherds?

Pick an adult Venture Buddy, and ask the following questions of that adult. Feel free to cut the adult off before complete answers are given.

• Where are your sheep? Did you lose them? That'd be a bad thing, if you lost them. You might lose your job.

• How come there are so many shepherds in one place at one time?

Listen, I hear what you're telling me, but here's what I think: I think you're all *Associate* Shepherds. You're just learning, so you don't have any sheep yet. You haven't graduated and gotten your sheepskin.

Besides, that really doesn't matter. What matters is that a bunch of angels—a whole *flock* of them—well, they were in the sky, and the baby was in a feed trough, and Mary was sitting in a stable along with Joseph… Look, I know I'm rambling. How about you just come with me and I'll show you. I'll take you to where the baby is. It's not far.

The Shepherd will then lead Venture Teams out of the meeting area to the predetermined location where a CD player will already be playing "Sheep Sounds" (track 11 on the *BibleVentures: Jesus—Manger Miracle* CD).

While the children are out of the meeting room, Joseph and Mary will transform it by setting up the Nativity scene, lighting candles, turning off the lights, and lighting the twinkling Christmas lights taped to the ceiling. Then Mary and Joseph will take their positions, waiting to be "discovered" by the children. Joseph will also turn on track 13 "Closing for Drama Center: Animal Sounds" on the *BibleVentures: Jesus—Manger Miracle* CD.

The Shepherd will continue his monologue with the Associate Shepherds as follows:

I was somewhere around here when the angels showed up. See how Bethlehem is over there on that hillside? And see where we had a campfire going?

Well, we were just enjoying a quiet night, talking about the stars, and keeping an eye on that crazy sheep, Buddy—he's the one who's always wandering off. He's a troublemaker, because he's always trying to talk the other sheep into escaping. Where they'd go, I don't know. Nothing out there but hungry wolves and bears. But Buddy is always muttering to the other sheep, then looking over his shoulder to see if we were listening.

You ask me, it's about time to have Buddy over for *lunch*, if you know what I mean.

Hey, how many of you Associate Shepherds like to eat sheep? Show me your hands if you've eaten a sheep lately. Not many of you—good. The sheep will like that.

The Shepherd will turn, as if yelling a short distance to shepherds who are with the sheep on the CD. **Hey, guys, I'll be right there! I'm just telling these Associate Shepherds what happened...Yeah, I know they don't have any sheep yet...they're still in training, *that's* why.**

Look, kids, turn and wave over there to the guys, will you? I think they're worried you're from the government, here to collect sheep tax. Show them you're friendly. Thanks.

Anyway, Charlie—he's one of the shepherds—was complaining about his ankle hurting. He twisted it when he ran down into a gully to grab Buddy and bring him back to the flock. Well, Charlie's complaining and we're talking and then—BAM!—this bright light appears, and we have to cover our *eyes* it's so bright.

Cover your eyes like there's something bright shining in them. Good.

Now fall to your knees like we did. Good.

Now start shaking and quaking in fear like we did. Good! It was *exactly* like that! OK, you can just sit on the floor now.

Then, out of nowhere, this angel appears!

I know, it sounds crazy—but it happened. Right here! And it's like this angel can read our minds because he says, "Don't be afraid!" It was a *talking* angel! Can you imagine?? I looked around, thinking I'd gone nuts, but all the other shepherds saw it and heard it too.

And you know what? We really *were* afraid! You woulda been too!

The Shepherd will turn, as if yelling a short distance to the shepherds on the CD. **Hey, Charlie, watch Buddy down there—he's starting to dig an escape tunnel again.**

Let's see, where was I? Oh yeah, the angel.

Then the angel said, "I bring good news. The Savior has been born in Bethlehem. You'll know it's him because he'll be wrapped in a cloth and lying in a manger."

That didn't sound like a savior to me, but who am I to argue with an angel? And then all of a sudden there are all these other angels—hundreds of them, maybe thousands of them, all singing and celebrating. It was amazing!

And then—they were gone. Gone back to heaven, I suppose.

Well, me and the boys headed for Bethlehem, and we looked around awhile and we found a stable. And there was the baby, just like the angel said. Just a minute...

The Shepherd will turn, as if yelling a short distance to the shepherds on the CD. **Look, I don't care *what* Buddy says—he's not digging for buried treasure. It's an *escape* tunnel! Just take the shovel and put it someplace he can't *reach* it!**

There we were, a bunch of shepherds with no sheep, wandering around town looking for a baby. People must have thought we were nuts. But we found him—and I can take you there. Come on...

The Shepherd will lead the children back to the room, but on the way the Shepherd will encourage kids to "walk like shepherds."

If you're gonna be shepherds, you've got to *walk* like shepherds. You've got to be quick on your feet, ready for anything. You've got to keep looking around so if a wolf or lion is coming, you see him a long way off. OK, let's see you walk like that...

Now, you've also got to walk in a confident way—to show the sheep who's boss. Let's see you walk confidently...

Finally, you've got to whistle to yourself a little. So do all that you were doing, and do a little whistling, too.

Outside the door to their meeting room, where inside Joseph and Mary are waiting, the Shepherd will caution the children to be quiet.

This is the spot. It's just like the angel said. Maybe it doesn't look like much—just a poor young couple with a baby. Just a stable. Just a feed trough. But that's if you're looking with your eyes. If you look with your heart, you see something else altogether.

The Shepherd will usher kids into the room, but not too close to the manger scene, then speak softly.

If you look with your heart, you see a special baby...you see a special gift from God.

Me and the other shepherds, well, we knew that  Jesus had come for us and we could share the good news. We knew we were standing in the presence of God himself.

After awhile, we went out into the streets and told everyone! We wanted to share the good news. Some people didn't believe us, but you do, I can tell. I can tell that you see with your hearts too!

Thanks for listening to my good news—it's time to get back to those sheep—Buddy's probably caught in a thicket somewhere, bellowing his head off, or he's got the other shepherds tied up.

As for you Associate Shepherds, go on up and talk to Joseph and Mary there. (To leader of the Venture Center) You, too.

They've seen a lot of shepherds tonight already, but they'll be happy to see a few more. Walk on up, and kneel near the baby.

See you soon. Peace to you...and joy to the world!

The Shepherd will leave the room as you lead the children closer to the manger and kneel.

When you and the children are near Mary and Joseph, they'll take note of you.

SAY **Mary, Joseph, may we visit with you for a few moments?**

Mary will answer: **Of course. You must be more shepherds. Tell us what you've been doing this night.**

Encourage children to stay in character as Associate Shepherds and to tell Mary and Joseph about their encounter with the Shepherd and what the Shepherd shared with them.

Here are questions for Mary and Joseph to use in prompting interaction with the Associate Shepherds:

• **What do you like most about being shepherds? What do you like least?**

• **What have you heard about our baby, Jesus?**

• **Jesus came for all of us. How might you share that good news—and who will you share it with?**

After children answer these questions, have Mary suggest the baby needs some sleep, and have her thank the Associate Shepherds for visiting.

Play "Instrumental Music for Prayer Time" (track 12 on the *BibleVentures: Jesus—Manger Miracle* CD).

Venture view

If there's extra time after groups discuss sharing the good news of Jesus, encourage groups to use the time to thank God for Jesus in prayer. The setting—gathered around a candle—is one that can encourage prayer.

Thank Mary and Joseph, then ask Venture Teams to move out into the room away from the manger area. Give each Buddy a lit votive candle in a holder. Ask groups to circle up with their Buddies, sitting on the floor. In each group, the candle will provide reassuring light and help the children focus.

Ask groups to discuss this question.

ASK

• **What are ways we can share the good news about Jesus? What gets in the way of our sharing it?**

While Venture Teams work, have Mary and Joseph extinguish their candles, gather props, and slip from the room.

When you have about one minute before needing to move children back to The Depot for the closing, raise the room lights and place a small sticker or stamp in the circle on each child's Venture Visa page. It's the page that shows Jesus in a manger.

Ask your children to look at the picture of Jesus in the manger. Ask your children to consider what a gift Jesus is in their lives.

Close your Venture Center with a short prayer, thanking God for giving us the gift of Jesus and letting us share that good news with others. Then help BibleVenture Buddies escort the children back to The Depot for the closing.

Jesus came for us, and we can share BP the good news!

Venture Verse: "For God so loved the world that he gave his one and only Son, that whoever believes in him shall not perish but have eternal life" (John 3:16).

Welcome!

You'll be leading the Art Venture Center for the next four weeks.

One great piece of news is that preparing for the four weeks is easy because you prepare just *one* week's lesson—and present it four times!

Here's how your Venture Center works: Each week children gather at The Depot for a time of opening and adventure. While at The Depot, children will get together in their Venture Teams, and then one group (it could be one Venture Team or several, but each will have an adult or teenage leader) will travel to your Venture Center.

This group of children will stay with you for 40 minutes and then return to The Depot for a time of closing and celebration.

In the weeks that follow, different groups of children will come to your Venture Center. You'll repeat the same activity for all four weeks, each week with a different group of children. This allows you to prepare just once and have four weeks of meaningful interaction with children as you lead them closer to God!

Your Venture Center

During this BibleVenture, children explore the birth of Jesus. Children will learn that BP Jesus came for us and we can share the good news.

You'll notice that the Point, BP Jesus came for us, and we can share the good news, is mentioned several times in your lesson. That's by intent, and it's important you reinforce the Point by saying it each time—or even more often. By

the end of this BibleVenture, children will have learned that Jesus came for us and we can share the good news.

In your Venture Center, children will use art to discover more about the birth of Jesus. Children will craft a stocking ornament which will hold a prayer they can pray with their families before exchanging gifts at Christmas. They will have many choices as they create their very own keepsake.

Your enthusiasm for this Venture Center and the art project will be passed on to the children (and BibleVenture Buddies!) you meet each week. Greet them with excitement, encourage them to be creative, and have fun together!

And be sure that you read ahead and plan for your Venture Center. Planning ahead and arriving early are both keys to leading a successful center!

Preparation

String small white twinkle lights across the ceiling. Either tie several lights together, or hang a lit star in one corner. Decorate a small Christmas tree, and wrap some empty boxes as gifts to put under it.

You'll also need these supplies:
- Bible
- matches
- scissors
- hole punch or other tool to make a small hole in the felt stockings
- several fine-tipped permanent markers
- craft glue
- two stocking shapes cut from various colors of felt, about 6 inches tall, 3½ inches wide at the top, and 5 inches wide at the toe, for each child
- 3-inch squares of felt in various colors
- white marabou boa (small in diameter), cut into 3½-inch sections
- a bowl of spangles, small metallic stars, and other shiny decorations that can be glued to felt stockings
- 6-inch piece of small gauge gold wire (22 gauge) for each child
- decorative beads (include a variety of colors and shapes) in bowls; one bowl for each team
- markers or crayons
- photocopy of the "Christmas Gift Prayer" for each child
- an appropriate sticker or stamp (one portraying a gift, if possible) to use in each child's Venture Visa
- CD player
- *BibleVentures: Jesus—Manger Miracle* CD

Because of time restrictions, it's best if you prepare a stocking for each child by cutting out the stocking and hot gluing the seams together before children arrive. This also removes the need to place hot glue guns into the hands of children, which is *never* a good idea!

As an alternative, you can sew the stocking together. In field tests, craft glue worked fine for decorating the stocking but couldn't withstand little hands repeatedly putting the prayer scroll in the stocking, then pulling it out again. Because this is meant to be a family keepsake, sturdy construction is a good idea.

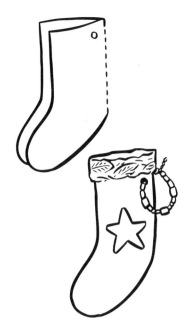

Make a copy of the prayer on page 61 for each student. When you photocopy the prayer on page 61, please don't enlarge it; it's sized so it fits easily into the stocking once it's rolled into a "scroll."

Place supplies on a table, and create a tray of beads and wire for each Venture Team.

Light the incense a few minutes before children enter the room. Be sensitive about selecting incense that's not overpowering—especially if you're in a small room or a room with poor air circulation.

The Venture Center

Have music playing as children arrive. You can use the Christmas music in your *BibleVentures: Jesus—Manger Miracle* CD or substitute a favorite CD or tape of your own.

Cut the stocking on a fold rather than in two separate pieces for a stronger stocking.

Also, hot glue will hold the felt together much better than any craft glue. Since the children will be storing their prayers inside the stocking, it needs to be durable.

Welcome children as they enter your Venture Center. Explain that kids will explore the events surrounding Jesus' birth by creating an art project they'll take with them for the enjoyment of their entire family.

SAY **Circle up with your Venture Buddies, and discuss this question.**

ASK

• **What's the best gift you've ever received?**

Allow several minutes for teams to talk, then draw attention back to yourself using your attention-getting signal.

Ask children to open their Venture Visas to the page that shows wise men with gifts for baby Jesus. Ask children to write or draw the best gift they've ever received in the space provided.

As children do this, place a stamp or sticker on the page to indicate the children have visited your Venture Center.

SAY **We often see Christmas plays and storybooks that show the wise men from the east showing up to visit Jesus while Jesus is still in the stable.**

In truth, we aren't exactly sure _when_ the wise men showed up. Jesus might have been a baby or even a toddler. But we do know two things for certain: The wise men brought gifts, and their arrival was a surprise!

Ask a volunteer to read Matthew 2:1-2, 9-12 aloud.

SAY **The gifts the wise men brought were gifts fit for a king.**

Gold was valuable then, just as it is now. Frankincense was made from tree sap and used as perfume or incense, and it was expensive too. Incense is what you smell in this room.

Myrrh is also made from tree sap. It's used as a perfume, spice, or incense. It has a bitter smell. Gold, frankincense, and myrrh were expensive gifts fit for royalty.

The wise men offered good gifts—_great_ gifts even—but God gave the world the greatest gift of all: Jesus! (BP) Jesus came for us, and we can share the good news.

Today, you'll make an ornament to hang on a Christmas tree. It will contain a prayer to share with your family before you open your Christmas gifts.

If your family doesn't use a Christmas tree, hang this ornament on a doorknob or somewhere else your family can see and enjoy it. And pick a time during the Christmas season when you'll pull out the prayer and share it with your family.

Read the following prayer aloud.

A Christmas Gift Prayer

Thank you, God, for gifts! And thank you for people with giving hearts, like those gathered together here.

You gave us the greatest gift of all when Jesus came for us.

Thank you for loving us enough to send your Son to save us from sin.

Thank you for your gifts of grace and forgiveness.

We pray that we'll live so everyone we meet will come to know about your great gift of love. Help us to share the good news of Jesus with others, today and every day.

In Jesus' name, amen!

You'll be able to change the prayer to put it in your own words if you'd like.

But make sure as you reword it—if you do so—you don't lose the truth in the prayer. God *did* give us the best gift ever when Jesus came for us. Jesus is the reason we celebrate Christmas with gifts!

Have children circle up with their Venture Buddies, who'll help kids complete the ornaments. Encourage your Venture Buddies *not* to make an ornament so they can focus on the children.

It's important to note that this isn't a rush-through-the-craft-project-and-make-it-look-like-the-leader's-project sort of activity. In fact, it's not a craft project at all. Rather, it's an *art* project.

You and your kids have a substantial amount of time to complete this project—so take it. Give kids the opportunity to move through the steps at their own pace. Some kids will zip through most of the steps, and others will focus on the details. Both approaches are fine. You can prod the children whose perfectionist tendencies get in the way of their completing the project and engage the done-too-soon kids in conversation about their projects.

And keep in mind that what the children create must reflect their own thoughts and feelings about God's gift of Jesus. This is a great opportunity to find out what your kids believe...but for that to happen, you must create a safe place for children to express themselves.

The point: Take your time. And let kids find ways to express themselves.

The following 10 steps will guide you through the art project.

1. Prepare the stockings ahead of time.

It may seem counterintuitive to do this portion of the art project for children, but think of it as preparing a canvas before an artist draws a masterpiece. It won't curb the creativity of your children.

You'll need a stocking cut from felt, about 6 inches tall, 3½ inches wide at the top, and 5 inches wide at the toe, for each child. You can use one color for all the stockings, or provide various colors. The upside of having a variety of colors is that you'll give children a chance to each choose the color he or she likes best.

The downside is that you may run out of a favorite color. Making felt stockings all the same color allows you to avoid arguments about colors.

Thinking about how your kids relate, determine how you'd like to handle the stocking-color decision.

Use the sketch on page 55 to create a template for your stockings. Again,

using hot glue to keep the sides together provides a stronger seam than using other types of glue.

2. Ask children to select a stocking.

You can invite children to come to the supply table to select one, or if stockings are all the same, you can distribute them. Either way, the remainder of your instructions will make more sense if children have the stockings in their hands when you're talking.

Caution: In spite of your best gluing efforts (and only the truly inspired are going to stitch up each and every stocking with an actual needle and thread), these stockings aren't made for children sticking their hands in up to their elbows and pretending the socks are puppets. Communicate to children these aren't playthings; they're art projects and must be treated gently.

3. Invite Buddies to go to the supply table to get scissors and felt squares.

Safety scissors, of course; and the 3-inch felt squares should be a variety of colors. Encourage Buddies to take a variety of colored squares with them so children have several options.

If you have a small group of children, allow them to each select their own square and let the Buddies collect the scissors.

4. Ask children to cut a shape out of the square that reminds them of Jesus and glue the shape on one side of the stocking.

That shape could be a star, since a star gave direction to the wise men, or a heart because Jesus loves us. The shape could be a cross because Jesus died for us. Children might cut out a profile of Jesus. Any shape that's meaningful for a child is an appropriate shape. Don't be overly concerned that the shape be "Christmassy."

Encourage BibleVenture Buddies to interact with children as the children select a shape that speaks to each child. Children are notoriously critical of their own artwork; so help Buddies encourage children regarding their efforts.

5. If they wish, let children each select a boa strip and glue it to the top of the stocking or add additional felt elements to the front of the stocking.

This isn't a requirement, but some children may wish to do this. Tell children they'll be writing on the front of the stocking, so they'll want to leave room to write their name and the year on the back of the stocking.

This is a wonderful opportunity for children to let their visual creativity run wild. They can add glitter, stars, and spangles to personalize their stockings.

Allow each child to do as much—or as little—as he or she likes to create a stocking that the child thinks reflects him- or herself.

6. Help children punch holes as indicated in the illustration.

Caution: Avoid placing holes too near the edges of the stockings. Each stocking will have one hole punched in it. Make the holes as small as possible. See the sketch on page 55 to guide you in placing the holes.

7. Give children each a piece of wire, and show them how to put one end through the hole and secure it by wrapping the wire around itself.

You'll have a tight loop holding the length of wire to the stocking and a long piece of wire sticking out.

8. Make a variety of beads available to each team, and encourage children to string together on the wire beads that remind them of their lives.

Children may look at you blankly. A bead reminding them of their lives?

Suggest that a bead may remind them of their lives because of the color—perhaps the color of a feeling a child has felt often lately (the red of anger, or blue of sadness). A yellow bead might be added because the child loves sunshine, or a green bead because green is the child's favorite color.

It can be the shape, especially if you've included designer beads.

It can be the number of the beads—perhaps five of them strung together because there are five people in the child's family.

It may be the size of the beads—three large ones and a small one next to the large ones because the child loves spring, summer, and fall...but hates winter.

Don't prescribe how a child goes about selecting beads and arranging those beads; it's the open-ended nature of this step that allows for the child to reflect on his or her life.

9. Help children secure the loose end of the wire to the loop they've already made.

This keeps the beads on the wire in a loop. Tuck the sharp edges of the wire so nobody gets poked!

10. Give each child a copy of the "Christmas Gift Prayer" to decorate and/or revise.

Children have a couple of options at this point. They can simply create a border around the piece of paper you've given them using markers and crayons, or they can turn the piece of paper over and write their *own* "Christmas Gift Prayer."

Visit a craft store, and for a few dollars you can add beads that reflect children's interests: sports, hobbies, and school activities. Mix these "designer" beads in with a variety of colored beads and beads of different sizes and shapes.

If they choose to write their own, children can base their prayers on the prayer you've given them, or start from scratch. Remind children that the prayer will be read to their families and, hopefully, for years!

After children have decorated and/or created Christmas Gift Prayers, ask children to put their names and the date on the back of their ornaments with a permanent marker.

When children have nearly completed their projects, ask BibleVenture Buddies to circle up with their teams and encourage children to one at a time give a "guided tour" of their beads, explaining what each one means.

Then ask teams to discuss these questions.

ASK • **You all made stockings, but each stocking is unique. In what ways are you unique?**

• If you could place any gift you wanted in a stocking for yourself, what would it be? If the gift could be for your family, what would it be?

• If you could give any gift to Jesus, what would it be? Why do you think Jesus would want that gift?

SAY **The wise men offered the first Christmas presents, but their expensive gifts weren't the best gifts of all. The best-ever gift was Jesus!**

Jesus came for us. That's such good news that I *want* to share it with others!

In the book of John, chapter 3, verse 16, that good news is summed up for us: "For God so loved the world that he gave his one and only Son, that whoever believes in him shall not perish but have eternal life."

Jesus is truly the gift that keeps on giving. When we love and obey him, we get to be with him forever!

The art project you just made is a gift that will last awhile too. Ask your parents if you can read the prayer just before your family opens gifts this year. Then put the prayer back in the stocking and decorate your tree with this ornament this year—and every year.

Close your Venture Center with a short prayer, thanking God for giving us the gift of Jesus and letting us share that good news with others. Then help BibleVenture Buddies escort the children back to The Depot for the closing.

Make life easy for your BibleVenture Buddies and yourself by making a copy of the questions for each leader. Then you won't have to keep interrupting the discussion flow to ask the next question.

If there's extra time after the art project and group discussion, encourage groups to talk about how they can give themselves to God. What can they do to become a gift to God or others?

A Christmas Gift Prayer

Thank you, God, for gifts!
And thank you for people with giving hearts,
like those gathered together here.
You gave us the greatest gift of all
when Jesus came for us.
Thank you for loving us
enough to send your Son to save us from sin.
Thank you for your gifts of grace and forgiveness.
We pray that we'll live so
everyone we meet will come
to know about your great gift of love.
Help us to share the good news
of Jesus with others, today and every day.
In Jesus' name, amen!

Venture Center Three:  The Games Center

Jesus came for us, and we can share the good news!

Venture Verse: "For God so loved the world that he gave his one and only Son, that whoever believes in him shall not perish but have eternal life" (John 3:16).

Welcome!

You'll be leading the Games Venture Center for the next four weeks.

One great piece of news is that preparing for the four weeks is easy because you prepare just *one* week's lesson—and present it four times!

Here's how your Venture Center works: Each week children gather at The Depot for a time of opening and adventure. While at The Depot, children will get together in their Venture Teams, and then one group (it could be one Venture Team or several, but each will have an adult or teenage leader) will travel to your Venture Center.

This group of children will stay with you for 40 minutes, then return to The Depot for a time of closing and celebration.

In the weeks that follow, different groups of children will come to your Venture Center. You'll repeat the same activity for all four weeks, each week with a different group of children. This allows you to prepare just once and have four weeks of meaningful interaction with children as you lead them closer to God!

Your Venture Center

During this BibleVenture, children explore the birth of Jesus. Children will learn that **BP** Jesus came for us and we can share the good news.

You'll notice that the Point, **BP** Jesus came for us, and we can share the good news, is mentioned several times in your lesson. That's by intent, and it's important you reinforce the Point by saying it each time—or even more often. By the end of this BibleVenture, children will have learned that **BP** Jesus came for us and we can share the good news.

In your Venture Center, children will use games to discover more about the birth of Jesus. This center is very much fun and games for the children, but along the way, they'll dive into the story of Jesus' birth and think about the amazing gift God offered us that first Christmas.

Your enthusiasm for this Venture Center and the games played will be passed on to the children (and BibleVenture Buddies!) you meet each week. Greet them with excitement, encourage them to join in the games, and have fun!

And be sure that you read ahead and plan for your Venture Center. Planning ahead and arriving early are both keys to leading a successful center!

Establish a nonverbal signal to direct kids' attention back to yourself. Suggestions: Clap your hands, flick the lights, or blow on a wooden train whistle or other unusual sound maker that won't be mistaken in the midst of discussion. Practice the signal several times until kids recognize it and respond to it.

Consider stringing several large jingle bells together to serve as a signal in this Center. They're bright, cheery, and seasonal!

Preparation

Before children arrive, gather these supplies:

- CD player
- *BibleVentures: Jesus—Manger Miracle* CD
- sets of "Eleven Questions" cards (p. 76)
- "Good News Headlines" (p. 75)
- cellophane tape
- large marshmallows
- dry spaghetti
- a stamp or stickers to place in children's Visas

Photocopy the "Eleven Questions" sheet, and cut the cards apart so you have a set of questions for each BibleVenture Team. Also, make enough copies of "Good News Headlines" to accommodate all your BibleVenture Teams after you've cut them apart.

Have Christmas music playing as children enter the room—any of the songs on the *BibleVentures: Jesus—Manger Miracle* CD will work well.

The Venture Center

Welcome children as they enter your Venture Center. Explain that kids will explore the events surrounding Jesus' birth and do it in a fun way.

SAY **First, let's listen to how the Bible describes the birth of Jesus in Bethlehem. But before we do, I want you to decide if you'd rather be a sheep, a shepherd, a wise man, or an angel.**

Allow children to decide, then continue.

SAY **Each of you has a motion to make whenever the character you picked appears in this story. All of the motions are silent motions—so don't say anything, just do the following.**

Demonstrate these actions, and ask your children to each practice their character's action a few times.

Sheep: Raise both hands and open your mouth and eyes wide, as if you're terrified.

Shepherd: Look scared and fall facedown on the floor.

Wise man: Stroke your beard and nod sagely.

Angel: Cup your hands as if they're a trumpet and you're shouting good news.

Play "The Christmas Story" (track 14 on the *BibleVentures: Jesus— Manger Miracle* CD). Encourage children to do the motions they've practiced at the appropriate times. If you and another reader wish to read the script live, it is provided on pages 70-74.

When the track has ended, ask children to circle up with their BibleVenture Buddies.

SAY **Great job acting out the motions for those personalities in our Bible narrative. I say "narrative" because it's more than a story—this really happened. Jesus was really born in Bethlehem, and angels announced his birth to shepherds.**

We acted out the sheep, shepherds, wise men, and angels, but who else was present for this event who we didn't act out?

Expect to hear about Mary, Joseph, and Jesus, and perhaps the innkeeper and King Herod, depending on how much your kids know about the events surrounding Jesus' birth.

Eleven Questions Game

Distribute the "Eleven Questions" cards that you've photocopied and placed in sets. Give one set to each BibleVenture Buddy.

SAY **Each of your Buddies has a set of cards that each lists one person or object that was part of the events surrounding Jesus' birth. Your Buddy will tape your card to your back. Don't peek—everyone else will be able to see your card except you.**

Your job is to ask your partner up to 11 questions that can be answered "yes" or "no" that will help you figure out what's written on your card. Your 11th question must be a guess as to who or what you are.

If you and a partner would rather perform "The Christmas Story" live, the script is provided for you, beginning on page 70.

For instance, I might start by asking if I'm alive. If the answer is "yes," I might ask if I'm a person. If the answer is "yes," I might ask if I'm a male. The idea is to narrow down who you are, or what you are.

Don't give anyone hints about who or what he or she is; just answer questions. And you'll have to keep track of how many questions you've asked. When you get to 10, make your 11th question a guess as to your identity.

Give Venture Buddies time to tape the cards on the backs of their team members. Then encourage kids to find partners, check out what's on the back of their partners, and start guessing!

After kids have discovered their identities, have Venture Buddies retrieve the cards and discuss these questions with their teams.

ASK

• **What made this easy or difficult for you?**

• **If your character was a person, how do you think he or she felt about Jesus' birth? Why?**

• **If you—not the character you're playing—had been in Bethlehem at the time of Jesus' birth, do you think you'd have known about Jesus' birth? Why or why not?**

After teams have had an opportunity to discuss these questions, draw attention back to yourself by using your attention-getting device.

SAY **If you were an angel or a shepherd, you'd have known all about Jesus' birth...and you'd probably have done what they did: tell someone!**

But most people in Bethlehem probably didn't know about what was happening in the stable out back of the inn. They didn't know because nobody told them.

That's true today, too: Some people don't know about Jesus because nobody has told them. **Jesus came for us, and we can share the good news!**

Ask children to take out their Venture Visas and turn to the page that shows shepherds running and shouting.

SAY **The shepherds used the best way they knew to communicate: They talked to people! How would you like to share the good news about Jesus? Write or draw your idea in the space on your Visa page.**

As children work, circulate through the room, placing a stamp or sticker on their Visa pages to indicate they've been in your Venture Center.

SAY **Let's practice telling other people good news!**

If children are finding it difficult to discover who or what they are in just 11 questions, give them a "bonus" number of questions to help them be successful. Keep the game fun!

Make life easy for your BibleVenture Buddies and yourself by making a copy of the questions for each leader. Then you won't have to keep interrupting the discussion flow to ask the next question.

"One way I can share the good news is..."

Told and True Game

Ask teams to line up single file, by order of birthdates. That is, someone born January 21st would be ahead of a person born February 3rd, and so on.

If in your teams you have more than five students, form smaller groups or combine extra students from several groups to make another team. You need to have an equal number of students in each group, preferably five or four students plus a BibleVenture Buddy.

SAY **There have been a lot of times in history where there was good news to share. The best news ever was Jesus' manger miracle, but there have been other good news moments too.**

In your group of five, you're going to take turns sharing good news, and you'll do it without using words. That's right: You're going to *act out* the good news and see if your teammates can guess what your message is.

Ask teams to form circles, with the person who was first in line going first, then following the birth order of participants.

Distribute the "Good News Headlines" so each person has one (including BibleVenture Buddies!) and no two people in a group have the same headline. If possible, distribute the headlines so teams sitting right next to each other don't have identical headlines.

Give each person two minutes to try to communicate his or her headline. After the game, ask teams to circle up with their Buddies and discuss these questions.

ASK

- **Why is what you shared a piece of "good news"?**

- **Why is Jesus coming for us good news?**

- **What's the best way to share the good news about Jesus?**

- **What's easy about sharing the good news about Jesus? difficult?**

Here's What the Good News Looks Like Game

For this game you'll need to give each team 30 marshmallows and 30 pieces of raw, dry spaghetti.

Ask teams to identify who on each team is wearing the most blue. That person will become the Team Sculptor.

SAY: **Team Sculptors, your job is to go to the far side of the room along that wall** (indicate a wall). **Turn your back to the rest of us and, using 15 marshmallows and 15 pieces of spaghetti, create an artistic masterpiece. Use the spaghetti to connect the marshmallows in as creative a fashion as possible...so long as you don't take more than two minutes.**

Ready? Go!

While the sculptors work, ask each team to identify who has the birthday closest to Christmas. That person will become the team's Second Sculptor.

SAY **Second Sculptors, your job is to exactly duplicate the sculpture that's being created over there by your Team Sculptor. That's a hard job, because even though you have the same materials—15 marshmallows and 15 pieces of spaghetti—you can't see what your Team Sculptor is doing. Sit down and face this wall that's opposite the one where your Team Sculptor is working.**

The rest of you on the team will line up single file between the Team Sculptor and the Second Sculptor. *Your* **job is to take turns running down there to see what the Team Sculptor has done and telling your team's Second Sculptor how to make the exact same thing.**

Here's the catch: You can only talk for 10 seconds when you get back to talk to your team's Second Sculptor. Then the next person in line runs down and looks and comes back with another 10 seconds of instruction.

Is everyone in position?

Team Sculptors, have you completed your masterpieces? You've got another 60 seconds to make something *amazing.*

Use the 60 seconds to make certain everyone understands his or her job. When 60 seconds have passed, tell the first "runners" from each team to go see what the Team Sculptor has created, then to dash back to give 10 seconds of instruction while the next runner dashes down to look.

This game can begin to drag after about five minutes, so keep it moving and when five minutes have passed, have teams compare the two sculptures created by their sculptors. How closely did the Second Sculptor come to replicating what was created by the Team Sculptor?

Ask teams to discuss these questions.

ASK

• **How well did we do making the sculptures look alike?**

• **What helped us be successful? What hurt our success?**

Ask for volunteers to share their teams' answers about what helped and hindered their success.

SAY **Without someone to carry the message from your Team Sculptor to your Second Sculptor, there would have been no way to be successful. The messages carried by people who had seen the sculpture were important!**

It's like that when we're telling others about Jesus. If we know and follow Jesus, we can tell others what Jesus means in our lives. We can tell others about the good news that Jesus came for them.

That's the good news: BP Jesus came for us, and we can tell others!

It should be about time for you to help BibleVenture Buddies escort children back to the closing program, but if there's still time to play, consider filling the time with the following game.

If you've still got time to play...

Extend your time by inviting teams to work together to disassemble their sculptures and use the materials to create...

• the tallest free-standing structure,

• the strongest structure (as measured by placing coins or other weight on the structure,

• the structure most like the Eiffel Tower, or

• the tippiest-but-still-standing structure.

The only rule: Everyone on a team must somehow touch the project as it is created!

These are provided for your reference. They're on the CD; you don't need to reproduce them.

The Christmas Story

Narrator 1

In those days Caesar Augustus issued a decree that a census should be taken of the entire Roman world...

Narrator 2

What's a decree?

Narrator 1

A decree is an edict.

Narrator 2

Oh.

Narrator 1

And everyone...

Narrator 2

What's an edict?

Narrator 1

It's a law. Caesar Augustus was the king over all the Roman Empire, and he wanted everyone counted.

Narrator 2

Got it. Thanks.

Narrator 1

No problem. And everyone...

Narrator 2

What sort of name is "Caesar Augustus"? I mean, if some kid had been named Caesar Augustus at *my* school, he'd have been laughed at non*stop.*

Narrator 1

Trust me: Nobody laughed at the king. At least not when the king could hear it. Can we carry on with this story?

Narrator 2
Oh, sure. Sorry. Didn't mean to interrupt.

Narrator 1
Fine. And everyone went to his own town to register...

Narrator 2
One last question, though...

Narrator 1
Yes?

Narrator 2
Wouldn't it have been easier for Caesar to let everyone stay home and just go door to door to count people?

Narrator 1
Maybe, but that's not what he did. He had everyone go back to the town where their family was from, and they signed in there. Is that all right with you? Do you want to go call Caesar and tell him to organize things differently?

Narrator 2
No, no...man, I didn't know you'd be so touchy about a simple question...

Narrator 1
Let's just move on, shall we?

Narrator 2
Sure.

Narrator 1
And everyone went to his own town to register. So Joseph went up from the town of Nazareth in Galilee to Judah, to Bethlehem the town of David, because he belonged to the house and line of David. He went there to register with Mary, who was pledged to be married to him and was expecting a child.

Narrator 2
That child would be Jesus, right?

Narrator 1
Right. We'll get to that.

Narrator 2

Just wanted you to know I sort of read ahead.

Narrator 1

Good for you, but perhaps not everyone *else* read ahead.

Narrator 2

OK. My favorite part is when the wise men show up with gold, Frankenstein, and myrrh.

Narrator 1

(Pause) I'll just clear that up when we get to it.

(Deep breath) While they were there, the time came for the baby to be born and she gave birth to a son. She wrapped him in cloths and placed him in a manger, because there was no room for them in the inn.

Narrator 2

They shoulda made reservations.

Narrator 1

And there were shepherds living out...

Narrator 2

We always make reservations when *we* go on vacation...

Narrator 1

Good for you. And there were shepherds living out in the fields, keeping watch over their flocks at night. An angel of the Lord appeared to them, and the glory of the Lord shone around them, and they were terrified. But the angel said to them, "Do not be afraid. I bring you good news of great joy that will be for all the people. Today in the town of David a Savior has been born to you; he is Christ the Lord...You will find the baby wrapped in cloths and lying in a manger."

Then, suddenly, many more angels appeared. They praised God and said, "Glory to God in the highest, and on earth peace to men on whom his favor rests."

Narrator 2

What happened to the sheep?

Narrator 1

The sheep?

Narrator 2

Yeah, if the sheep were sleeping and wham! there was an angel hanging in the sky, wouldn't the sheep get scared and run off?

Narrator 1

The Bible doesn't really *tell* us what happened to the sheep.

Narrator 2

Poor sheep...

Narrator 1

But the Bible *does* tell us what happened to the shepherds.

Narrator 2

Really? Tell me about *that*.

Narrator 1

I'd be glad to.

When the angels left the shepherds, the shepherds said to one another, "Let's go to Bethlehem and see this thing that has happened." So they hurried off and found Mary and Joseph, and the baby, who was lying in the manger. When they'd seen the baby, the shepherds spread the word concerning all that had been told to them about this child.

Narrator 2

(Pause) That's it?

Narrator 1

Um...yes.

Narrator 2

What about the wise men? What about the gold, Frankenstein, and myrrh?

Narrator 1

We know they came to find Jesus—the book of Matthew tells us so—but we aren't sure *when* the wise men showed up. They may have visited when Jesus was a baby, or maybe when Jesus was a toddler.

Drama Script

Narrator 2

But they brought *cool* gifts.

Narrator 1

That they did. Gold, frankincense—not *Frankenstein*, by the way—and myrrh. All expensive gifts fit for a king.

Narrator 2

Why do you think people call them the "wise men"?

Narrator 1

I'll tell you why I call them the wise men.

Narrator 2

Why's that?

Narrator 1

Because they looked for Jesus. Anyone who looks for Jesus is wise as far as *I'm* concerned.

GOOD NEWS HEADLINES

World War II Is Over!

RED SEA PARTS AND GOD'S PEOPLE CROSS SAFELY!

TORNADO MISSES TOWN!

Man Lands on Moon!

Lazarus Raised From Dead by Jesus!

The Sky Is Not Falling!

RECORD CROPS FEED MILLIONS!

GOLD DISCOVERED!

God Answers Prayer!

Earth Is Round—Sailors No Longer Fear Falling Off Edge!

Eleven Questions

Angel	**Manger**	**Joseph**
Cloths used to wrap baby Jesus	**Shepherd**	**Shepherd's staff**
Mary	**Baby Jesus**	**Gold**
Myrrh	**Caesar Augustus**	**Census**
Bethlehem	**Wise man**	**Good news of great joy**

Venture Center Four:

Jesus came for us, and we can share the good news!

Venture Verse: "For God so loved the world that he gave his one and only Son, that whoever believes in him shall not perish but have eternal life" (John 3:16).

Welcome!

You'll be leading the Cooking Venture Center for the next four weeks. One great piece of news is that preparing for the four weeks is easy because you prepare just *one* week's lesson—and present it four times!

Here's how your Venture Center works: Each week children gather at The Depot for a time of opening and adventure. While at The Depot, children will get together in their Venture Teams, and then one group (it could be one Venture Team or several, but each will have an adult or teenage leader) will travel to your Venture Center.

This group of children will stay with you for 40 minutes and then return to The Depot for a time of closing and celebration.

In the weeks that follow, different groups of children will come to your Venture Center. You'll repeat the same activity for all four weeks, each week with a different group of children. This allows you to prepare just once and have four weeks of meaningful interaction with children as you lead them closer to God!

Your Venture Center

During this BibleVenture, children will explore Jesus' birth. Children will learn that 🅱🅿 Jesus came for us and we can share the good news.

You'll notice that the Point, 🅱🅿 Jesus came for us, and we can share the good news, is mentioned several times in your lesson. That's by intent, and it's important you reinforce the Point by saying it each time—or even more often. By the end of this BibleVenture, children will have learned that Jesus came for us and we can share the good news with others.

In your Venture Center, children will cook and make discoveries about Jesus' birth. Children—even the boys—love creating something they'll eat themselves. Your kids will also dig into the Venture Verse for this unit, John 3:16.

You don't have to have an oven in your room to do any of these projects, but at least one of them requires that you have easy access to an oven in your vicinity. After preparing the Brown Sugar Oat Squares, an assistant or a BibleVenture Buddy can take the pan(s) to the kitchen for the brief cooking time.

Your enthusiasm for this Venture Center and the interactive cooking you'll do with the children will be passed along to the kids (and BibleVenture Buddies!) you meet each week. Greet everyone who comes into your Venture Center with warmth, encouraging them to join in the fun.

A note: We've tested these recipes, and at least in our test kitchen they worked well. If you're at a particularly high or low altitude, or there's a factor that impacts cooking in general in your area, you'll have to make the same accommodations for these recipes that you do in your other cooking.

Do this: Test these recipes at home before you do them at your BibleVenture. Running through them once will increase your confidence and give you a better idea of quantities you'll need for your program.

Also, whenever you serve food to children, you need to be sensitive to food allergies and issues. Nuts, fruit, glutens, sugar, artificial flavorings and color—any of these have potential to trigger a reaction. Know what is and isn't safe to serve your kids before you put a plate of goodies in front of them.

Consider providing parents with a copy of the recipes you'll use and ask if any of the ingredients are a problem for their children.

Preparation
Before children arrive, gather these supplies:
- Bible
- drinking cups, one for each child
- pitchers of water
- a stamp or stickers (a smiling face if possible) to place in children's Visas

You'll also need to:
- arrange for use of an oven and a microwave
- buy the ingredients for each of the recipes you decide to use (see individual recipes on pages 85-86 for lists of ingredients)

To lead this Venture Center, you'll need the church kitchen (assuming you're meeting at a church), so inquire early what supplies you're allowed to use, and make sure you've reserved the kitchen during your meeting times.

It's important to have clean hands and easy cleanup, so be sure there's ample soap and paper towels at the nearest sink. Have a liquid hand sanitizer available too.

Experiment with melting chocolate in the microwave you'll actually use so you have the system down cold. Packages provide information on time required, but that's not good enough: You also need to be sure you're using the *medium* power setting on the microwave. We've experimented and discovered that using a higher setting will burn rather than melt chocolate. Microwaves vary, so the settings you use at home won't necessarily work on the church microwave.

A tip: If you don't overheat the chocolate, you can always reheat it just before it's used. If you can't tame the church microwave, you can start the process at home and then simply reheat the chocolate in the church kitchen.

You'll also be organizing a food preparation station for each team, so allow time to measure ingredients into paper bowls or cups. It will be very advantageous to have a helper with you, someone who can quickly clear away empty containers and set up new food preparation stations as children come and go. Give your helper a damp rag, a broom, and a garbage bag.

Before children arrive, preheat the oven to 375 degrees; you want the oven to be ready to slide in pans of oat squares.

It will reduce stress and make your Venture Center easier if you do whatever work you can in advance. For instance, you'll be giving each child four pretzel sticks on wax paper; there's no reason you can't set those out all at once.

And a final tip: Make a sample edible Nativity scene. Children don't need to make theirs look just like the sample, but it will give them an idea of how the project might look.

The Venture Center

SAY **Welcome to the Cooking Center! We're going to learn more about Jesus' birth as we cook up some fun and tasty treats.**

But before we do anything else, let's take care of kitchen hygiene: It's time to wash our hands.

Ask BibleVenture Buddies to help assure that children do a good job of washing their hands at the sink, or using liquid hand sanitizer.

Establish a nonverbal signal to direct kids' attention back to yourself. Suggestions: Clap your hands, flick the lights, or blow on a wooden train whistle or other unusual sound maker that won't be mistaken in the midst of discussion. Practice the signal several times until kids recognize it and respond to it.

Consider stringing several large jingle bells together to serve as a signal in this Center. They're bright, cheery, and seasonal!

Brown Sugar Oat Squares

SAY **Jesus lived a long time ago, and in a different part of the world from where we're standing. The food he ate was different from what you usually eat.**

In Jesus' day, and in that part of the world, people ate lots of dried fruit and vegetables. They had no way to refrigerate food, so meal preparation was more of a challenge for them. Today we'll make a simple, sweet treat that may be a little like the foods Jesus and his family ate.

Set up multiple stations for food preparation—one for each team. At each station have the ingredients pre-measured and in separate bowls or cups. This requires multiple pans and mixing bowls, as well as a lot of paper cups, but it's worth the effort to let members of teams cooperate together to create their snacks.

Ask BibleVenture Buddies to assign each child on their teams an ingredient from the recipe. Any child who doesn't have an ingredient will be a "mixer"—and that's a duty that can be shared by several children.

Ask children to add their ingredients into the mixing bowl.

After all ingredients have been added, have the Mixers take over and press the mixture into the bottom of an ungreased 9x13 pan. Send the pans to the kitchen to cook for eight minutes in the preheated 375-degree oven.

While the treats are cooking, move ahead to the next activity. Allow children who want or need to wash their hands to do so before moving ahead.

Chocolate-Dipped Pretzels

SAY **In your teams, take two minutes to discuss these questions.**

ASK

• How close do you think Jesus wants to be to you, and why do you think that?

After two minutes have passed, ask for volunteers to share what they heard in their teams.

SAY **It sounds like you think Jesus is looking for a close friendship with you. That's true. In fact,  Jesus came for us, and we can share the good news!**

Ask teams to come up to the place you've laid out the pretzels on wax paper and for each child to take one of the sets of four pretzels and wax paper then return to sit with his or her team.

Avoid stampedes by releasing teams one or two at a time to retrieve their pretzels.

Candy melts will melt more smoothly and at a lower temperature than chocolate or almond bark. Candy melts can be found in the cake decorating section of many department stores, discount stores, and craft stores.

If you choose to use milk chocolate, see page 84 for instructions.

After children are seated, using oven mitts to carry the container of melted chocolate, take the chocolate to teams so children can dip their pretzels into the melted chocolate. Instruct children to dip pretzels only halfway then to lay the dipped pretzels on the wax paper to set.

After children have finished, set the chocolate aside.

SAY **How close is the chocolate to the pretzel? That's how close Jesus wants to be to you!** **Jesus came for us, and we can share the good news!**

After the chocolate cools a bit more, it will be stuck to the pretzel for good! Each one of you has made two to eat in a little while, and two to share. Be sure to tell the person who you share your pretzels with that **Jesus came for us, and we can share the good news!**

If you think the proximity of the pretzels will be too much of a temptation, ask children to carefully carry their creations to a table off to one side of the room for storage. Be sure each child somehow indicates (on a piece of paper or sticky note) which pretzels are his or hers.

Edible Nativity Scene

Before children arrive, create trays of the items listed on the "Edible Nativity Scene" recipe page (page 85), plus a section of newspaper. Ask teams to each send a representative to get a tray from the part of your room where you've placed the prepared trays.

When team representatives return to their teams, ask them to spread out the newspaper to be a work surface where children will work.

SAY **Find a partner in your team, and tell that person where you were born. The town and, if possible, which hospital.**

Allow a minute for partners to share their information, then ask a volunteer to read Luke 2:7 aloud.

SAY **If Jesus had been your partner, he'd have told you he was born in Bethlehem, and that there was no hospital. Instead, there was a stable.**

We don't know exactly what the stable where Jesus was born looked like. It may have been a cave, or it may have been a barn of some sort. Use your graham crackers to create a stable on your plate. Use icing as glue to hold the crackers together. Remember to leave a door for your stable, and keep half of a graham cracker to use later.

Give children time to accomplish this task.

ASK

• What do you think might have been scattered on the floor of that stable so the animals had a soft bed to sleep on?

Most of your children haven't had experience with stables, but it's likely they'll mention straw or hay.

SAY **Hay is often used in stables. Let's make some hay out of these shredded wheat biscuits. Crumble your biscuit over your plate, then gently place the hay in the stable, and around the stable entrance.**

Demonstrate how to do this. It's important children realize they can crumble the biscuits without launching cereal shrapnel all over the room.

Reread Luke 2:7 aloud.

ASK

• What did Jesus rest in?

Ask for volunteers to describe what a manger is.

SAY **That's right: A manger is what we now call a feed trough. It's where the food for animals was put. Let's make a manger for our Nativity scene by putting two single crackers together to form a V. Use the icing as your glue to stick them together and to the plate.**

Give children time to accomplish this task. As they work, ask teams to discuss these questions.

ASK

• How do you think your mother would have felt if she'd had to give birth to you in a barn? What might she have said?

• Why do you think God would let Jesus be born in a stable?

After teams have had a few minutes to talk, gather attention back to yourself using your attention-getting device.

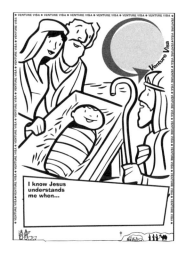

SAY **Let me read another passage from Luke, chapter 2.** Read aloud verses 8-11.

Jesus was God's Son, the Savior of the world! And *still* God let Jesus be born in a barn! But it wasn't a lack of love or bad planning—it was so we'd know that Jesus understands us. He understands us when we're poor...when we're tired...when we're humble.

Ask children to open their Venture Visas and turn to the page that shows the manger and Mary and Joseph looking down at their new baby boy.

SAY **I'm glad Jesus came for us. And I'm glad Jesus understands us. I can tell he understands me when Jesus forgives me for being grumpy. In the space on your page, write or draw a way that you know Jesus understands you.**

As children work, move around the room, putting a stamp or sticker on each child's Visa page to indicate the child has visited your Venture Center.

Sharing Good Food and Good News!

By the time children finish the edible Nativity scene, the Brown Sugar Oat Squares will be cooked and ready to bring back to the room.

Ask the Venture Buddies to help cut the squares and distribute napkins to their teams, and for children to set aside their Nativity scenes.

Ask a volunteer BibleVenture Buddy to lead everyone in a short prayer, then have Buddies place an oat square on each napkin as children retrieve their chocolate-covered pretzels.

SAY **Feel free to eat two pretzels and the oat square on your napkin. The rest of the chocolate-covered pretzels and oat squares will go into your resealable bag so you can take them home to share with a family member or a friend. Just remember to share this with your family member or friend too:** **(BP)** **Jesus came for us, and we can share the good news!**

Make cups and water available for children.

Encourage teams to discuss the following as they enjoy their snacks.

ASK

- **What did you like best about cooking together today?**

- **How is sharing our snacks like sharing the good news about Jesus?**

SAY: **One of my favorite Bible verses is found in the book of John, chapter 3, verse 16: "For God so loved the world that he gave his one and only Son, that whoever believes in him will not perish but have eternal life."**

That verse reminds me that Jesus came for us. That's good news for me! If it's good news for you but you don't know Jesus, we'd love to help you meet him. Talk with your BibleVenture Buddy, or feel free to talk to me later.

It should be nearly time to return to the closing program. If you have a few additional minutes at this point, invite BibleVenture Buddies to discuss these questions with their teams.

Make life easy for your BibleVenture Buddies and yourself by making a copy of the questions for each leader. Then you won't have to keep interrupting the discussion flow to ask the next question.

Getting a plate covered with graham cracker structures and crumpled wheat biscuits home in one piece is a challenge for children. Increase the odds by covering individual Nativity plates with cling wrap.

If you want to make the manger more detailed, offer the children some animal crackers to add as stable animals.

Make copies of recipes you use for the children to take home. They will love cooking with their families, and it will encourage them to share the lessons they learned from you!

ASK

- **Why do you think it's important to know about Jesus?**

- **Why do you think it's important to know Jesus?**

- **How can you tell if you know Jesus?**

How to Melt Chocolate for the Pretzels

Melting chocolate requires a bit more than just tossing a bag of chocolate chips into a microwave. Here's how to get best-ever results...

Put the chocolate chips or coarsely chopped milk chocolate in a microwavable container. Place the container in a microwave set to *medium*. You can't just "nuke" chocolate; it melts more effectively at lower temperatures. If you doubt that, leave a chocolate bar on the dash of your car this summer and come back in five minutes. A gentle heat (no more than 115 degrees) is all that's needed.

Watch the bowl in the microwave carefully. Once the chocolate turns shiny and has begun to liquefy (this should take between a minute and four minutes, depending on the type of chocolate you've used), remove it, then stir the melting chocolate by hand to keep it smooth and silky.

Keep stirring the chocolate gently until children are ready to dip pretzels into the chocolate. If you let the chocolate sit, the milk solids and fat will begin to separate; you'll end up with a grainy, lumpy chocolate stew.

If something happens and you *do* end up with a chocolate lump, add a bit of vegetable oil to make the chocolate smooth and shiny again. Realize this will impact the flavor, though, so be sparing with the oil.

This is most definitely a process to practice before you do it at the BibleVenture program.

Chocolate-Dipped Pretzels

This list of ingredients makes a batch for one BibleVenture Team.

- one-cup microwave-proof measuring cup

- microwave

- 14 oz. candy melt—dark chocolate or white chocolate
  —one bag for every two BibleVenture Teams

- large pretzel sticks

- wax paper

- resealable plastic sandwich bag

Edible Nativity Scene

This list of ingredients will supply one BibleVenture Team.

- large shredded-wheat biscuit, one per child

- can of icing

- graham crackers, three whole sheets per child

- paper or plastic plate, one per child

- plastic knives, one per child

- bear-shaped graham crackers (optional)

- animal crackers (optional)

Brown Sugar Oat Squares

This list of ingredients makes a batch for one BibleVenture Team.

- 1½ cups packed light brown sugar
- ½ tablespoon baking powder
- 3 cups regular oats
- ¾ cup melted butter
- ¾ teaspoon vanilla
- 9x13 pan

- mixing bowl
- fork to mix
- measuring cups
- measuring spoons
- resealable plastic bag—one per child

Song Lyrics

Mary's Boy Child

Long time ago in Bethlehem, so the
   Holy Bible say,

Mary's boy child, Jesus Christ,

Was born on Christmas Day.

(Chorus)

Now Joseph and his wife, Mary,

Went to Bethlehem that night,

And found no place to lay their head,

Not a single room was in sight.

(Chorus)

While shepherds watched their flocks
   by night,

They saw a bright, new, shining star.

And from the East there came three
   men

Bearing gifts from afar.

(Chorus)

(Chorus)

Hark now, hear the angels sing:

A new King born today

That folks may live forevermore

Because of Christmas Day.

Joy to the World!

Joy to the world!

Joy to the world!

Joy to the world!

Joy to the world!

Joy to the world!

The Lord is come!

Let earth receive her King!

Let every heart prepare him room,

And heav'n and nature sing,

And heav'n and nature sing,

And heav'n and heav'n and nature
   sing.

Joy to the world!

Joy to the world!

(Repeat verse)

Silent Night

Silent night! Holy night!

All is calm, all is bright.

'Round yon virgin mother and Child.

Holy Infant so tender and mild,

Sleep in heavenly peace,

Sleep in heavenly peace.

Three Wise Men

Three wise men,

Three wise men,

Follow the star,

Follow the star.

They got on their camels, and off they went

With gold and myrrh and frankincense.

We all admire the reverence of three wise men.

Song Lyrics

O Come, All Ye Faithful

Come on! Let's go!

Come on! Let's go!

Come on! Let's go!

Come on! Let's go!

O come, all ye faithful, joyful
and triumphant,

O come ye, O come ye, to Bethlehem.

Come and behold him,

Born the King of angels.

O come let us adore him.

O come let us adore him.

O come let us adore him.

Christ, the Lord.

Yea, Lord we greet thee,

Born this happy morning.

Jesus, to thee be all glory giv'n,

Word of the Father,

Now in flesh appearing.

O come let us adore him.

O come let us adore him.

O come let us adore him.

Christ, the Lord.

O come let us adore him.

Christ, the Lord.

Let's go! Come on!

Let's go!

Away in a Manger

Away in a manger, no crib for a bed,

The little Lord Jesus laid down his
sweet head.

The stars in the sky looked down
where he lay,

The little Lord Jesus asleep on the
hay.

The cattle are lowing, the Baby
awakes,

The little Lord Jesus, no crying he
makes.

I love thee Lord Jesus! Look down from
the sky

And stay by my side until morning is
nigh.

Be near me Lord Jesus! I ask thee to
stay

Close by me forever and love me, I pray.

Bless all the dear children in thy tender
care

And fit us for heaven to live with thee
there.

Into My Heart

Into my heart,

Into my heart,

Come into my heart, Lord Jesus.

Come in today;

Come in to stay;

Come into my heart, Lord Jesus.

Into my heart,

Into my heart,

Come into my heart, Lord Jesus.

Come in today;

Come in to stay;

Come into my heart, Lord Jesus.

Jesus Is All the World to Me

Jesus is all the world to me,

My life, my joy, my all;

He is my strength from day to day;

Without him I would fall.

When I am sad, to him I go.

No other one can cheer me so.

When I am sad, he makes me glad;

He's my friend.

Jesus is all the world to me,

My life, my joy, my all;

He is my strength from day to day;

Without him I would fall.

When I am sad, to him I go.

No other one can cheer me so.

When I am sad, he makes me glad;

He's my friend.

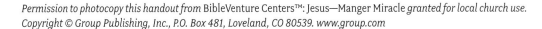

Song Lyrics

We're So Glad That You Were Born

We're so glad that you were born,

'Cause if you were not here,

We would not see your smiling face

Nor hear your voice of cheer.

It's hard to say, "God bless you!"

To someone who doesn't exist!

Especially on your birthday,

You would certainly be missed.

So happy, happy birthday

From friends who think you're dear!

And if the Lord should tarry,

We'll be singing to you next year.

My Jesus, I Love Thee

My Jesus, I love thee,

I know thou art mine.

For thee all the follies of sin I resign.

My gracious redeemer,

My Savior art thou.

If ever I loved thee, my Jesus 'tis now.

My Jesus, I love thee,

I know thou art mine.

For thee all the follies of sin I resign.

My gracious redeemer,

My Savior art thou.

If ever I loved thee, my Jesus 'tis now.

Job Description: BibleVenture Buddy

BibleVenture Buddies have the joy—and the challenge—of connecting with kids in a deep, significant way.

As a BibleVenture Buddy, here's what you'll become to the kids in your care...

A trusted friend. You're a grown-up who's glad these kids came, who knows their names, who's been praying about what's important to them. Your focused attention and listening ear help your kids realize they're important to you—and to God.

A role model. How you interact with kids sets the tone for how they'll interact with each other.

A guide. Instead of being the "teacher" with all the answers, you're someone who asks great questions. You jump in and enthusiastically do the activities *they* do at BibleVenture. You gently guide kids as they discover how to apply God's Word to their lives and enter into a deeper relationship with Jesus.

A steady influence in kids' lives. From week to week, you're there with a smile and kind word. You don't demand that kids perform to earn your approval. You don't give kids grades. You're in their corner, dependably cheering them on.

And as you serve God and the kids on your Venture Team, you'll help Jesus touch kids' hearts and change their lives—forever.

To be a spectacularly successful BibleVenture Buddy, it helps if you...
- love God,
- enjoy being with children,
- can be reflective and thoughtful,
- are comfortable talking with children about Jesus,
- believe children can understand and live God's Word,
- are accepting and supportive of children,
- model God's love in what you say and do, and
- like to laugh and have fun.

Responsibilities

As a BibleVenture Buddy, your responsibilities include...
- attending any scheduled training sessions,
- greeting children as they arrive,
- accompanying your Venture Team when traveling to a Center,
- joining in activities with your Venture Team,
- encouraging the kids on your Venture Team,
- facilitating discussions in your Venture Team,
- actively seeking to grow spiritually and in your leadership skills,
- assisting Center Leaders as needed,
- overseeing the sign-out sheet for your Venture Team, and
- praying for the children you serve.

Job Description: BibleVenture Center Leader

BibleVenture Center Leaders provide fun, engaging experiences for small groups of kids. Because the focus of each Center is slightly different, the skills required to lead each center will vary from center to center, too.

But there are a few things *every* effective and successful Center Leader has in common. Successful Center Leaders...

- love God,
- enjoy and value children,
- are energetic and upbeat,
- maintain a positive attitude,
- can organize and motivate children to listen,
- are humble,
- are observant,
- attend scheduled leader training,
- prepare lessons thoroughly and with excellence, and
- model God's love in what they say and do.

Responsibilities

At the BibleVenture Center program, Leaders serve in these two areas:

1. The Depot

The Depot Leader is the "up front" leader, helping kids transition into BibleVenture by leading a brief, fun, upbeat program.

You're responsible for...

- collecting necessary supplies,
- preparing and leading the weekly openings and closings with excellence,
- reinforcing the Bible Point as you lead,
- leading music, or finding someone to help you do so, and
- praying for the children and BibleVenture Buddies you serve.

2. Venture Centers

Venture Center Leaders encourage kids to form lasting relationships with their BibleVenture Buddies, small-group members, and Jesus by leading an excellent 40-minute lesson.

You're responsible for...

- collecting necessary supplies,
- preparing and leading the weekly program with excellence,
- reinforcing the Bible Point as you lead,
- asking questions that will be discussed among the small groups (not with you!),
- cleaning up your area after your lesson, and
- praying for the children and volunteers in your BibleVenture program.

Job Description: BibleVenture Servant Leader

BibleVenture Servant Leaders support the BibleVenture program by jumping in to help where needed. You have a few assigned tasks but will probably do far more as you're asked to substitute for a missing BibleVenture Buddy, help out with a drama, gather supplies, or...

Successful BibleVenture Servant Leaders...

- love God,
- enjoy and value children,
- are energetic and upbeat,
- maintain a positive attitude,
- are humble,
- are observant,
- attend scheduled leader training,
- have servant hearts, and
- model God's love in what they say and do.

Responsibilities

As a BibleVenture Servant Leader, your responsibilities include...

- attending any scheduled training sessions,
- greeting children as they arrive,
- staffing the Depot ticket window during the opening and closing times,
- encouraging kids and leaders,
- actively seeking to grow spiritually and in your leadership skills,
- assisting Center Leaders as needed, and
- praying for the children and leaders in your BibleVenture program.

BibleVenture Sign-In and Sign-Out Sheet

We value the children trusted to our care! Please sign your child in and out. And if there are people who are not permitted to pick up your child, please provide that information to our staff.

CHILD'S NAME:	PERSON SIGNING CHILD IN:	PERSON SIGNING CHILD OUT:	Check if ONLY the person signing child in can sign child out.

Bonus Training Session!

High Impact Teaching—Teaching the Way Your Kids Learn Best

At your BibleVenture program this four weeks, you have a message to communicate that's critically important in kids' lives: that Jesus came for them, and that they can share that good news with others.

Those two truths sum up both the heart of the gospel and the Great Commission—arguably two of the very foundational stones of a strong faith in Christ.

And yet, you have just four hours to connect with kids and communicate those truths. With so much to communicate and so little time to make the connection, you can't afford to waste any opportunity.

This one-hour session will help you show your leaders how to better teach their kids—by teaching in the way that kids learn best.

At the end of this workshop, participants will be able to

• identify their own preferred learning styles,

• demonstrate an understanding of eight intelligences/learning styles (using the Quick Quiz), and

• share one practical step they'll take to personally apply this material in their roles at your BibleVenture program.

Supplies
- Bible
- name tags
- markers
- CD player
- *BibleVentures: Jesus—Manger Miracle* CD
- snacks
- copies of the "Intelligences Handout" (one per participant)
- auditory attention-getter
- signs: "Manual," "Poke Around," "Ask a Friend"
- 3x5 index cards (one per participant)
- pens
- copies of "Quick Quiz" (optional)

You'll be interrupting discussions between participants several times during this workshop. Decide now what signal you'll use to make those interruptions as inoffensive as possible. Flashing the lights is one option, but a stronger one is to select an audio signal such as blowing on a wooden train whistle or tapping on a block of wood. You want a signal that's easily heard but not as abrupt as a cymbal crashing through the room.

You'll note that at the end of this workshop there's a Quick Quiz. Use this if you want to know how effectively you've communicated the information in the workshop. If you intend to use the Quick Quiz, let participants know upfront so they can take notes.

Before the Workshop

Before participants arrive, place snacks where participants can easily access them. Also, create three small signs, and tape each one in a different corner of your room where the signs will be visible from the center of the room. You'll need signs that read: "Manual," "Poke Around," and "Ask a Friend."

Ask God to encourage your BibleVenture Leaders through you, and that participants will use what they learn to help kids grow closer to Jesus. Ask God to bless your leaders as they minister to children and other adult leaders.

Greet participants warmly as they arrive. Ask each person to fill out a name tag with his or her first name in capital letters and in lowercase letters, the name of someone who taught that participant an important lesson in lowercase letters. Mention that participants will be asked to share the story of who that person was and what the life lesson was.

After participants have gathered, ask them to be seated.

SAY **I'm so glad you're here! Let's start our time together with prayer.**

Briefly offer up the training time to God, and ask God to help each participant lay aside other concerns so he or she is open to learning and ready to apply what's learned.

SAY **Several times during our workshop, I'll ask you to talk with someone near you. When it's time to wrap up that conversation and for you to again focus on the front of the room, I'll use this as a signal.**

Demonstrate the signal you'll use.

SAY **When you came in, I asked you to write on your name tag the name of someone who taught you an important life lesson. Turn to someone who's sitting near you, and move your chairs so you can comfortably talk with each other. Then take a few minutes to share what that person taught you, and how. You and your partner will each have about 90 seconds to talk.**

When 90 seconds have passed, interrupt to explain that this would be a good time for those who haven't shared to begin telling about the person who taught them a valuable lesson.

When the final 90 seconds have passed, draw attention back to yourself with the auditory attention-getter you decided to use.

SAY **As you shared I wandered around and eavesdropped, and there are lots of ways people taught us important life lessons. There was a lot of diversity in the lessons and also in the teachers of those lessons.**

But there are at least two common threads that run through all of our stories: for better or worse, the people who effectively taught us important life lessons were somehow in a relationship with us, and the lessons were taught in ways that connected with us.

In my life, one of those effective teachers was...(share your own story here, taking care to do so in about 30 seconds).

Notice that my story is like yours: The teacher was in a relationship with me, and the lesson connected with me in a powerful way.

You've sat through countless sessions where someone wanted to teach you something. You've done that at school, at church, and some of you get regular sessions at work, too.

Yet you can recall just a fraction of the material that's been aimed in your direction. I'll bet there are classes you took where, thinking back, you can't even remember the teacher.

That's not because you're somehow inadequate as a student. The fact is that most teaching is completely forgettable because it falls short in at least two ways:

• There's no relationship between the student and the teacher, and

• There's no connection between the learner and the material.

The good news for us is that our BibleVentures program has relationship-building opportunities built right in. BibleVenture Buddies are all about relating to the children, and the Venture Center Leaders encourage relationship-building by directing teams to learn together and talk together. There are never any dry, dusty lectures in our program. Everything is relational.

But are we presenting Bible material in a way that truly connects with kids? What can we do to raise the odds that we make those critical connections with children?

Let's try a little experiment.

Italian Shoe Instructions

Ask workshop participants to each remove one shoe. When they've done so,

SAY **Now let's listen to some simple instructions. Please follow along.**

Play "Italian Shoe Instructions #1" (track 15) on the *BibleVentures: Jesus— Manger Miracle* CD.

The track lasts about two and one-half minutes, and unless you have someone in your workshop who speaks Italian, it's going to be a long, confusing few moments.

Inconspicuously slip your shoe back on as the track plays.

At the end of the track, turn to your workshop participants and point to your shoe, which is back on your foot.

SAY **I noticed that a lot of you didn't follow the directions given...what happened?**

Let workshop participants answer.

SAY **I gather that not a lot of us understand Italian, and that this exercise would have been far easier had you actually understood what was said. Let's hear the same instructions, in English this time. Follow along again, please.**

Play "Italian Shoe Instructions #2" (track 16) on the CD.

Once participants have their shoes back on, continue.

SAY **Turn to a neighbor and discuss these questions.**

ASK

• **How was our first try at this experience—listening to a language we didn't understand—like or unlike being in a class where you don't understand the material?**

• **How did you feel during that first round? during the second round—the one in English?**

Allow participants to share for a minute or two, then draw attention back to yourself with your audio attention-getter.

Ask for a few volunteers to offer insights that came from their pair-shares.

SAY **None of us would think it wise or appropriate to teach a session of BibleVentures in a language our kids don't speak. We know that children would quickly quit listening and grow frustrated** [substitute other negative feelings participants identified].

Yet, that's exactly what we do if we teach without considering the learning styles that God has wired into our children.

Let's take a look at how learning styles impact our own lives.

Sewing Machine Repair

Ask participants to stand in the center of the room. Once they're assembled there, continue.

SAY **Let's say that you're home and you've just realized you have a problem: Your sewing machine isn't working properly. You want to get it humming** along without jamming, and you know that at least in theory it's possible to make a few small adjustments and the problem will be solved.

Except you don't know what to do. You're willing to try to fix the sewing machine, but you need information. You've got to get some information and learn a bit before you try to fix the machine.

I'm going to suggest three ways you could go about getting the information. There are other ways, but let's keep it simple by giving you three options. I'm going to read through your choices once now, and I'd like you to listen to see which option is the one you'd most likely use to learn what you need to learn about fixing the sewing machine. I'll review the three options again after I've presented them once.

● Option 1: You'd consult the manual.

There's a lot of text and some diagrams that show the various components. You'll read through the relevant pages and consult the diagrams, then give it a shot.

● Option 2: You'd call someone who can talk you through it.

So long as you can get someone on the sewing machine help line to tell you what to do, you'll be fine. Where's that 800 number?

● Option 3: You'd open up the machine and poke around a bit.

You want to see what's what before you get too worried about specifics. Hey, is that a loose wire over there on the left?

Those three options again: You want to see the manual, you want to talk with someone, or you want to get your hands dirty looking under the hood of the sewing machine.

Don't analyze it too deeply or try to pick the "right" response. There is no right response; they all work fine as answers.

If you're a manual consulter, go stand in the corner with the sign that says "**Manual.**" Point out the correct corner.

If you're a person who'd want someone to talk you through the procedure, go stand in the corner with the sign that says "Ask a Friend."

If you're someone who'd open up the hood and poke around a bit to see if you can figure it out as you go, go stand in the "Poke Around" corner. And try to not touch anything you can break over there.

After everyone has moved, continue.

SAY **Notice that we have a bit of diversity here. We wouldn't all go about learning what we need to know the same way. And that's not bad. Each of these approaches can end up with a repaired sewing machine—it's just that we'd learn what we needed to learn differently.**

We all learn in a combination of ways, but it's typical that there's a dominant style method that we use most often.

Those of you in the "Manual" corner who read the manual and look at the diagrams are probably primarily visual learners. You take in information best by seeing it.

Those of you who are in the "Ask a Friend" corner are probably primarily auditory learners. You take in information best by hearing it. You benefit from lectures, audiotapes, and discussions—which are all ways of information reaching you through your ears.

And those of you in the "Poke Around" corner are likely primarily kinesthetic learners. You learn best by doing things. You're not afraid of trial-and-error approaches to fixing sewing machines, and you seem to learn well through your fingers.

Assuming you have enough leaders so there are at least two in each corner, ask the small groups of similar learners to discuss these questions.

ASK

• What sort of activities do you tend to enjoy when you're teaching? What sort of activities do you find less enjoyable? For instance, you might love games, but not enjoy lectures or crafts.

If you have a small group or there aren't enough leaders in one or more corners to at least have a pair-share, combine in whatever way will let everyone have someone to talk with.

After a few minutes of discussion, use your audio attention-getter to draw attention back to yourself. Ask participants to form a large group again, and distribute paper and pens to everyone. Suggest they might want to take notes when ideas strike them about how they can be even more effective at connecting with kids.

Learning Styles

SAY **Depending whose model you use, there are three learning styles...five learning styles...Howard Gardner of Harvard University has identified eight "multiple intelligences" that are essentially eight ways to resolve problems,** create products, and find or create solutions. In short, eight ways to be smart!

Let me quickly review the eight multiple intelligences identified by Gardner. As I describe them, think of someone you know who seems to be smart in this way.

● *Word Smart people...*

are the writers, readers, and public speakers of the world. They can tell stories, write poetry, or captivate a jury with a closing argument in court. Words come easily to them, and they're able to use those words to their advantage.

● *Bodily Smart people...*

are able to use their motor skills in ways that amaze us mere mortals. They might be athletes or dancers, actors or surgeons. Eye-hand coordination is usually highly developed, and they seem to be "naturals" because they learn quickly and perform well when bodily movement is involved.

● *Math and Logic Smart people...*

get their tax returns right on the first try. They're good with numbers, sequences, analysis, and organizing data. You might find these people gravitating toward accounting, mathematics, and science.

SAY **Let's stop here for a moment. Turn to a partner, and briefly describe someone in your life you identified as one of those three intelligences: Word Smart, Body Smart, or Math and Logic Smart.**

Share the person's name and what you see in that person that convinces you he or she falls into the category you've identified.

After participants talk for a few moments, continue.

SAY **Notice that we were talking about people who are smart in three different ways...but they were all smart. There's more than one way to learn—and it may not match the way we learn best.**

Let's take a look at five more ways to be intelligent and to learn.

• *Visual and Space Smart people...*

are the folks you want to call if you're looking to redecorate your house or to shoot your next music video. They have artistic sensibilities to spare and might enjoy drawing, sculpting, visualizing, and using their imaginations. The next time you talk to Pablo Picasso, congratulate him on being Visual and Space Smart!

• Interpersonally Smart people...

are able to make friends easily and find that they're sensitive to the feelings of others. These are the peacemakers, mediators, and politicians. They're able to empathize and see the world through the eyes of someone else. They often gravitate toward teaching, counseling, acting, and the pastorate.

• Nature Smart people...

are unusually aware of the natural world. Ecologists, zoologists, and your friendly neighborhood forest ranger may all be naturalists at heart—and head! They're able to sort and classify, and can explain how earthquakes really happen.

• Musically Smart people...

have a solid sense of rhythm. They're the people who often hum and sing to themselves; music just seems to touch them deeply. Want to get their attention? Put on a piece of music—even in the background—and you'll see their ears perk up. They may play an instrument or sing. They almost certainly enjoy listening to music.

• Intrapersonally Smart people...

are introspective souls and enjoy time to reflect and think. They have strong opinions and beliefs that have been thought through, and these are people who are often very capable when it comes to setting and meeting goals. Look for them in any field where ideas are important such as philosophy, theology, and psychology.

Whew! That's a lot of information to toss at you. Let's take a minute to digest it a bit more.

Turn back to your partner, and tell your partner which of those intelligences sounds most like you when it comes to learning. Because most of us have several primary ways we learn about the world, pick two that feel familiar. Explain to your partner how you see those strengths operating in your life.

I'll quickly list them again so you have time to choose two from the menu:

• Word Smart

• Bodily Smart

• Math and Logic Smart

- **Visual and Space Smart**
- **Interpersonally Smart**
- **Nature Smart**
- **Musically Smart**
- **Intrapersonally Smart**

Allow several minutes for participants to talk, then draw attention back to yourself with your audio attention-getter.

SAY **Let me read the list again. We might expect that because we all work with children in an educational setting, we'll tend to have the same two primary intelligences. But let's check.**

I'll read the list again, and I'd ask that you raise your hand when I mention one that you identified as a primary intelligence—and learning style—of your own.

Read the following list aloud. Take care to highlight the diversity of learning styles in the room.

- **Word Smart**
- **Bodily Smart**
- **Math and Logic Smart**
- **Visual and Space Smart**
- **Interpersonally Smart**
- **Nature Smart**
- **Musically Smart**
- **Intrapersonally Smart**

The Importance of Integrating Multiple Intelligences/Learning Styles

SAY **Note that while there are similarities, there are lots of differences, too. That's a good thing! It means we have depth and variety—the better to connect with kids who have the same learning styles!**

You'll note that in this BibleVenture, there are different primary learning styles addressed in the material.

- **The Cooking Center requires children to follow directions and interact with a recipe—which engages children who are Math and Logic Smart. The Bodily Smart children who learn best through hands-on experiences are also engaged.**

- **The Drama Center involves children who are Bodily Smart as well as Interpersonally Smart children.**

- **The Art Center grabs the attention of Visual and Space Smart children immediately, as well as Interpersonally Smart children as they discuss and debrief what they've done in the Center.**

- **The Games Center gives lots of learning styles an opportunity to engage, depending on the game.**

Throughout the program the Visas and Venture Teams capture the hearts and minds of Interpersonally and Intrapersonally Smart children, and each week Musically Smart kids get to sing and make music. And since Word Smart kids get to talk—a lot—they're engaged too.

About the only children who aren't specifically addressed in this BibleVenture program are Nature Smart children, and few if any children have this intelligence as their only (or primary) way to learn.

In short, if we'll use the program as it's designed, during the four weeks of this program every child will be engaged in deep Bible learning that's geared especially for that child! No child will be bored! And we leaders will be engaged too!

The Danger of Doing It Your Way

SAY **Think for a moment about a learning style that doesn't connect well with you. Do you have it in mind? Turn to a partner, and share what learning style is clearly not your first choice.**

After participants share for a moment or two, continue.

SAY **For me, that disconnected learning style would be** [fill in an intelligence/learning style that doesn't connect with you]. **If I were to be asked to teach a class that required me to use that style, I'd be lost. I'd probably change the material so I could teach out of a strength, rather than a weakness.**

It's a common temptation to make changes. If a leader who's not musically smart is asked to lead singing, it's tempting for that leader to cut the singing and substitute a drama or other approach to covering the material. The leader is more comfortable, and the class never knows what it's missing.

But what also happens is this: Children who have a musical intelligence are left out in the cold.

As I mentioned, our BibleVenture program covers a spectrum of intelligences and learning styles. If you change the ones used in your Venture Center, or in the opening or closing programs, we're no longer covering the major intelligences and learning styles. Kids get left out.

That's why it's important that you not change the basic approach used in your area. If you need to adapt the wording, fine. If you want to shift the activities into a new order, that's probably OK too.

But don't revise materials you've been given so you eliminate one or more of the intelligences that are used.

Right Person, Right Spot

SAY **Turn to a new partner, and in a minute or less explain what leadership role you play at our BibleVenture program. Describe what you do.**

After pairs have had up to two minutes to talk, use your audio attention-getter to draw attention back to yourself.

SAY **Now, with your partner, answer these questions.**

ASK

● **In what ways am I in the right job, given the way God has wired me with intelligences and learning styles?**

● **In what ways will I need to stretch to be effective in the role I'm filling?**

● **What's one insight I gained at this session about how I learn—and teach?**

● **What will I do with the insight I gained that will help me be more effective as a leader in our BibleVenture program?**

Draw attention back to yourself using the audio attention-getter.

SAY **We're not the only teachers who have had to adapt to effectively reach a group of people. Consider what the Apostle Paul wrote in 1 Corinthians 9:21-23:**

"To those not having the law I became like one not having the law (though I am not free from God's law but am under Christ's law), so as to win those not having the law. To the weak I became weak, to win the weak. I have become all things to all men so that by all possible means I might save some. I do all this for the sake of the gospel, that I may share in its blessings."

Before we leave, I'd like to make certain you don't lose hold of the insight you gained and your thoughts about how you'll put it to use to increase your effectiveness in our program.

Please jot down your insight and action step on a 3x5 card now.

Distribute pens and cards, and allow time for participants to write. Collect the pens and ask participants to hang on to their cards.

If you choose to use the Quick Quiz, distribute it, and ask participants to fill it in. Allow up to three minutes for this task.

Close with prayer, thanking God for the commitment of the participants to children's ministry in your church, and asking God's blessings for your program.

Distribute the "Intelligences Handout" as participants leave.

Encourage participants to linger for a few minutes enjoying snacks. This provides an opportunity for relationships to develop further and for friends to spend time together.

Howard Gardner (Harvard University) wrote a book in 1983 titled *Frames of Mind: The Theory of Multiple Intelligences.* That, and his later work, identified eight "intelligences" that help us understand that students learn in different ways.

Here are ways to be smart (categories of learning styles) that relate to those Gardner identified:

Word Smart

To these students, words come easily. They enjoy reading, writing, and discussing ideas. They also tend to be interested in and enjoy learning languages and mastering grammar and other word-related skills.

Bodily Smart

These students enjoy using their bodies. They like acting out roles and dancing, and they do well with movement and exercise. They often are strong in fine-motor skills.

Math and Logic Smart

These students are logical and do well with analyzing data and evaluating information. They're often strong in math skills and deductive reasoning.

Visual and Space Smart

Arts and crafts are fun for these students. They visualize things well and often enjoy the opportunity to design or draw what they've visualized.

Interpersonally Smart

These students value relationships highly and often make friends easily. They're generally able to work together well and able to organize others. Look for them to be sensitive to feelings of others and sometimes able to solve conflicts among peers.

Nature Smart

These naturalists are strong in observing life around them and unusually aware of the natural world. They enjoy classifying and categorizing and being in nature.

Musically Smart

These students enjoy creating music, performing, and learning about all things musical. They're easily engaged by interacting with music in a variety of ways—singing, playing, or listening.

Intrapersonally Smart

Usually introspective, these students are able to set goals and objectives and to work with priorities. They're often reflective and in touch with their own beliefs and values.

We want to learn how to better present information so it sticks. Help us by filling out this quick quiz! We discussed eight different intelligences and learning styles. Briefly describe what each one means.

Word Smart

Bodily Smart

Math and Logic Smart

Visual and Space Smart

Interpersonally Smart

Nature Smart

Musically Smart

Intrapersonally Smart

You identified one thing you could do that would enhance your effectiveness as a leader in our BibleVenture program. What was it?

Thanks for filling this out!

Jesus—Manger Miracle

BibleVenture Invitation Letter

Dear Katie,

Angels appear in a night sky, frightening shepherds...an ancient prophecy is fulfilled...a star hangs in the sky, leading foreign visitors to a king...

Sounds like a Hollywood movie, doesn't it?

Except this isn't a movie...it's something that really happened! And you can learn all about it!

You're invited to join us at our *Jesus—Manger Miracle* BibleVenture each Sunday night starting July 6 at 6 p.m.

We'll meet for four Sundays in a row—all July—and you won't want to miss a single night!

Each one-hour program will have you visiting a different BibleVenture Center. One week you may be acting in a fun, no-lines-to-learn drama presentation. Another night you may be crafting an art project to take home. There's always something different, and it's always fun!

Tell your mom or dad right now that you want to join your friends at BibleVenture on July 6! Circle the date on the family calendar! That's the date the adventure begins...and who knows where it will end?

It just might change your life!
Sincerely,

Audrey Ferris
BibleVenture Director
First Church
555-1212

Invite kids to your Jesus—Manger Miracle *BibleVenture program! Adapt this invitation to fit your schedule and church letterhead, then send a copy to each child in your Sunday school. Post copies on community bulletin boards, and send invitations to neighborhood children who visited your vacation Bible school, too!*

Please join us at our

BibleVenture™

program

At this time: _____

In this room: _____

for a celebration of good news!

We're glad Jesus came for us and wants us

to share that good news with others!

**For God so loved the world that he gave his
one and only Son, that whoever believes in him
shall not perish but have eternal life.
—John 3:16**